PAN
Tokyo

BONIN ISLANDS
IWO JIMA
MARCUS
OLCANO
SLANDS
MARIANA
ISLANDS
TINIAN • SAIPAN
• GUAM
ENIWETOK
TRUK
KUSAIE
CAROLINE
ISLANDS

WAKE

MARSHALL
ISLANDS
KWAJALEIN

GILBERT
ISLANDS
MAKIN
• TARAWA

SOLOMON ISLANDS
Rabual
NEW
BRITAIN
BOUGAINVILLE
EW
INEA
NEW GEORGIA
TULAGI
Port
Moresby
GUADALCANAL

CORAL
SEA

VANAUTU
FIJI

NEW
CALEDONIA

MW00638636

N

MIDWAY

HAWAIIAN
ISLANDS
Pearl
Harbor

JOHNSTON

PALMYRA

BAKER

QUATOR
EQUATOR

SAMOA
ISLANDS

NEW
ZEALAND

PACIFIC WAR MARINE

Clyde Holloway

So Many Books..., Inc.
Vancouver, Washington

Pacific War Marine

First Edition

Painting pg. 81: Sgt. Tom Lovell
Photos: pgs. x, 51, 136, 140: Holloway family collection

All other photos were copied at the National Archives, Washington, DC.
The captions enclosed by quotation marks accompanied the originals,
though some here have been abbreviated from the originals.

Book design: Anita Jones, Another Jones Graphics

Library of Congress Control Number: 2004099111

ISBN: 0-9759063-0-5

Printed in the USA

Dedication:

This book is dedicated to the memory of those United States Marines who served in the Pacific in World War II. May they never be forgotten.

ACKNOWLEDGEMENTS

Many people helped me while writing this book, some with technical assistance, but most with emotional and moral support. My heartfelt appreciation is extended to all who assisted me.

Of course, nothing would have been possible without the selfless efforts of my mother and father, Margaret and Stanley P. Holloway. My siblings, Dorothy Nilles, Anne Kannegaard, and David Holloway are always there with encouragement. Cynthia Holloway, of Cynthesis Studio, and my sister in law, was not only supportive, but was instrumental with technical advice and helped me see my writing as a book.

Others include, in no relative order, Jerry Fine, Ben Tiefenthaler, Bill Haas, Kurt Jensen, Bill Rees, Diana Wells, Susan Holton, of Great Northwest Book Promotion, Anita Jones of Another Jones Graphics, and Bob Smith of Book Printers Network.

Foremost in my gratitude is my wife, Beth, who is always able to fortify me with her genuine compassion. I would be remiss not to also mention our wonderful children, Brittany, Max, and Nick.

INTRODUCTION

What are the chances of going to lunch and finding something that will change your life? I had just finished my ham and cheese sandwich as I looked around the large lunch-break/conference table at Choice Medical. There were a few magazines lying haphazardly within reach and I grabbed the "Smithsonian." I leaned back in my chair to do a little reading before I went back to work. Checking the contents page, I noticed an article about the World War II battle of Tarawa, revisited after 50 years. This caught my attention because I knew my father had been there as a Marine and I also knew that it had been an exceptionally bloody battle.

The first part of the story recounted how the Marines slogged through low tide water while being mowed down by Japanese machine guns. Skimming over some of the text, I turned the page and stared into an old photograph. I sat as if paralyzed—looking back at me was my father in chest-deep water, clinging to a pier and desperately trying to advance to the beach while under machine gun fire. The determined look on his face was one I had seen many times when I was a boy watching my father working hard on the farm. But this was different. In the picture, Dad was just a few years past being a boy himself. He was a young man who wasn't sure he would be alive in the next five minutes.

After showing the photo to everyone in the office, I called "The Oregonian" columnist Margie Boulé, who interviewed me over the phone and wrote a column in the paper about my discovery. The response to the column was overwhelming. People had been touched by the story and many called or came by to tell me about their memories of that time. One man I had known *for years without knowing he had been in the war, told me, "I was over there too. We got the hell beat out of us." Margie Boulé received a call from a young man, Randall Clarke, from Portland, whose father, Elmo Clarke, was the other Marine in the picture. Elmo Clarke received the Silver Star for his bravery that day.*

As we were growing up, Dad didn't say very much about the war to my brother, David, my sisters, Dorothy and Anne, and me except for a few humorous anecdotes. What could he say? We were kids—none of us would understand. But it wasn't just us—after he came home nobody asked what happened over in the Pacific and he let those years sink into the back of his memory. He was content to let the history books tell the story. I, however, felt that writing down Dad's own first hand version would be a fitting tribute to him and all those marines who served with him. I wanted to write a book about Dad's war experiences. The question was whether or not Dad would feel comfortable recounting those years. I called my folks to ask both Mom and Dad if they would approve of my plans. If either one had said they had qualms about the idea, that probably would have been the end of it. Mom answered the phone and I told her about my idea of writing a book. She told me it sounded like an excellent idea, but, of course, I would have to ask Dad. "Just a minute, I'll put you on speaker phone." That's how phone conversations are conducted with my parents. They can turn up the volume and not worry about interference with their hearing aids. The phone screamed in my ear, then I heard Dad's booming voice, "How are you, son?"

"Well Dad, I'm scheming." I told him about my plan. Then I asked Dad if he would mind telling me about his part in the war. Without hesitation, he replied, "After 50 years it doesn't hurt to talk about it. I'll tell you all I can remember."

So started this book. I began making sojourns to my folks' home in Pullman, Washington, where Dad and I would sit at the dining table or in the front room and I would listen and record my father's memories of that time.

My father, Stanley P. Holloway, joined the Marines when the war broke out. There were over 500 men in his battalion. At the war's end there were only 17 men left of the original group that became known as "The Forgotten Battalion." My father was one of the 17 left standing when the smoke cleared. The battalion was used for island invasions throughout the war and they simply forgot to bring them home for almost four years, hence the name "Forgotten Battalion." When they were needed, which was often, their unit was attached to a different division for each combat landing: Tulagi and Guadalcanal—First Division; Tarawa—Second Division; Guam—Third Division; Saipan—Fourth Division; and Iwo Jima—Fifth Division. The individual commendations are too numerous to name, but the Forgotten Battalion earned six battle stars, five Presidential Unit Citations, and two Naval Citations.

———

Stanley P. Holloway's high school graduation picture. He was sixteen years old.

Stan Holloway in his Marine uniform

Chapter
ONE

Rubbing the sleep from my eyes, I directed my bare feet toward the kitchen, where Mom was preparing some breakfast. I had started from home, Vancouver, Washington, late in the evening and arrived in Pullman about 2 o'clock in the morning, read a fast chapter in my book, and slept like a baby until I was roused in the morning by the sound of activity in the kitchen.

Mom gave me a hug and kiss, "It's so good to see you, darling. Your father's been up in the garden. He'll be in in just a minute." I looked out the kitchen window, past the rose-lined deck, and saw Dad walking down the decline of lawn from the garden. His steps were short but he walked briskly as he approached the sliding glass door. I opened the door for him. "Hi, Padre" "Son, how are you?" His face beamed with a big smile as he extended his hand.

Staying with my parents is like relaxing at a bed-and-breakfast. The food is wonderful and the troubles of the world disappear. After breakfast Dad and I sat at the table and prepared to dive into our first interview session. Mom pulled out a nice tape recorder, which was much better than the one I had, and presented me with several blank tapes, before she left to work on one of her projects. "Dad, I want to proceed somewhat chronologically. So why don't you tell me about your first day in boot camp." Dad leaned forward, toward the mike, with both hands on the table. He looked at the tape recorder, then his eyes looked up from under his bushy eyebrows directly at me, "Okay, I remember that day well..."

Had they singled him out the moment he marched into boot camp? After all, at 22 years old he was older than most of the other recruits—many 16 or 17 years old. Stan Holloway had lived on his own, worked for a living, done his own cooking and laundry. Most of the other young men had just come from home, Mom and Dad, security, sharing a room with a brother. Dinner was served at six and the family would sit around the table and talk about their day. Being away from home and the folks was a new and frightening experience for them. This wasn't summer camp. The train ride from Seattle to San Diego had been exhilarating, but now they were here, at Marine Corps boot camp. This was wartime and they were all going to war.

The drill instructors (D.I.s) yelled at them to strip down to their skivvies (underpants). They shuffled the boys around from station to station, issuing them clothes, a duffel bag, and toiletries in a metal bucket. The cold floor on their nervous bare feet seemed to be announcing along with the drill sergeant, "Your life will never be the same from this moment on!"

"This is how you will make your bunk." The sergeant quickly demonstrated the proper procedure. "You have your bunk assignments, now MAKE THEM!"

This is where Holloway got into trouble. He began to make his bed—easy, nothing to it—while quietly whistling between his teeth. There was no prelude or warning.

"YOU LIKE TO WHISTLE?!!"

Startled, Holloway quickly wheeled around to attention. He was surrounded by sergeants, staff sergeants, corporals—everyone who had a stripe or more on his arm had been invited to this little impromptu party. Their wide-eyed dyspeptic expressions signaled that something, centering on Stan, was wrong. The D.I. grabbed the young man's bucket, dumped the toiletries on the floor, and in one movement, slammed the upside down bucket over Holloway's head.

"WHISTLE 'HOME SWEET HOME'!"

About six bars into that old country favorite—WHAM! Holloway thought his head had exploded. Then he realized the D.I. had hit the tin bucket with his swagger stick, a short metal-tipped cane, sometimes carried by officers and found to be very stylish (especially in vogue with the Nazis.)

"WHISTLE 'YANKEE DOODLE'!"

As the swagger stick hit the bucket, the sound concussion wiped out all other brain functions The pain screamed from his eardrums through the rest of his head. It was obvious the D.I. didn't really care about the quality of the rendition of the songs. Not once was Holloway allowed to even get close to the chorus. In fact, by the third song he had given up trying to simulate anything musical. The air forced between his teeth produced a strained sound that might have come from a musical recorder in the hands of an enthusiastic beginner.

WHAM! "CHANGE TUNES!"

Four years later, when in D.I. school, Holloway would learn that this was a calculated part of the training in boot camp. Rule Number 1: Show them who's boss. Rule Number 2: Never let them forget it. So here he was, part of the lesson plan on the first day of school. This little performance only took 5 or 10 minutes, but it would have a lasting impact on the new boys. They hadn't even been there 30 minutes and this poor chump had become the painful example of an object lesson. You could tell by the sickened look on their faces—God, I'm glad that's not me!

WHAM! "CHANGE TUNES!"

This wasn't exactly the scenario that Stan Holloway had pictured for himself the first day in boot camp. Growing up on a homestead near Roy, Idaho, Stan had learned to love and appreciate his country. He was a patriotic flag waver. He thought when he marched into boot camp, they'd give him a rifle and treat him like a person. If he was willing to die for his country, shouldn't he be treated with respect? No, fate and reality were collaborating to show him just how surprising life can be.

On December 7th, 1941, while the Japanese air force was destroying a major part of the U.S. Navy at Pearl Harbor, Stan and his younger brother, Wally, were kissing Mom and Dad goodbye. It had been a relaxing weekend visit in Amity, Oregon — playing pinochle and filling up on Mom's cooking. The boys promised they would be back soon. They jumped into Stan's 1935 gray Ford sedan for a leisurely drive up Highway 99 toward Seattle. Glen Miller's "In the Mood" wafted from the radio. The warm sun rays soaked into the brothers' dark brown arms lolling out the open windows. Stan was feeling content as he relaxed behind the wheel of his car. He was proud of his Ford. The light gray exterior was clean and polished. Fabric seat covers kept the soft interior looking pristine. It had four on the floor and a flat-head V-8 engine that Stan and his friend, Howard Thompson, had just rebuilt. There was one small feature that Stan especially liked about that car—it had chicken wire in the roof that acted as an aerial. That gave the radio excellent reception. And that radio was proving it as they cruised up the road. As they approached the town of Olympia, the music suddenly stopped.

"WE INTERRUPT THIS BROADCAST."

Japan had committed a sneak attack on the U.S. Navy at Pearl Harbor. President Franklin D. Roosevelt's voice was firm and strong as he declared, "WE ARE NOW AT WAR!"

Stan knew what he was going to do. He didn't have to think about it. He was young and strong, not married like Wally, and he loved his country. The only question was which branch of the service to join. At his present job with Bonneville Power he had become acquainted with Gill Banks, an older guy who told stories about being in the Marines in the war in Europe. Banks had been in the trenches and had been gassed by the Germans. He didn't tell Stan very much about that, but he did have some fascinating stories about being a Marine in foreign countries. So that settled it. He would join the Marines. Stan looked at Wally and said "Looks like I'll be joining up." Wally stared back at him, after Stan turned his head back to view the highway. Not usually at a loss for words, all Wally could utter softly was "Holy shit." Eight months later Wally would enlist in the Air Force.

"WHAM! 'SWANEE RIVER!'"

This was a turning point in Stan Holloway's thinking. He would always be patriotic. He would always love his country. But he refused to let the Marine Corps break him. He would maintain his inner dignity no matter what they did to him. From this moment, Holloway would be marking time until he could leave the Marine Corps behind. He had enlisted in the Marine Corps Reserve. That meant that he would actively serve for the duration of the war. He might be in for 6 months or maybe a year. The common joke was "We should be home by Christmas." Holloway could take whatever humiliating and degrading crap the Marine Corps had to offer, but when it was time to leave, he wouldn't tarry. He had no way of knowing that through the next four years, he would encounter a barrage of struggles, with not only the Japanese enemy, but the ravages of nature and disease. He would see death first hand; many of those around him severed from their bright futures. In four years, the essence of the U.S. Marine Corps would seep into his bones, with the feeling of "Semper Fidelis" at the very marrow of his being.

"GET THAT BUCKET OFF YOUR HEAD! CHOW IN FIVE MINUTES"

It was like emerging from a cave where you had been blindfolded and used for target practice. His ears rang like two perpetually loud tuning forks were stuck in them. But the lesson was over—mercifully. It seemed as if he had been under that bucket for an hour. It would be a long time before Holloway would see an empty bucket without feeling like kicking it.

That night Holloway crawled into his bunk exhausted. In the matter of seconds before slumber carried him away, he could hear a few small sounds drifting through the quiet of the large room—a bed creaked, someone coughed, and he could hear a recruit nearby quietly sobbing.

During the next couple of days the recruits settled into the rigors of training. Up before dawn and hitting their bunks well past dark, their days were taken up with marching on the hard blacktop, pushups, running, calisthenics, marching, and more marching. They were being trained to physically chase the Japanese from anywhere in the world back to Japan, taking breaks along the way to do push-ups. Every step of the drilling was accompanied by verbal instructions from the D.I., at a decibel level that seemed to exceed the limits of human vocal chords, and sometimes at a range of a few inches from a recruit's head. If anyone called his rifle a "gun" he was made to perform "up and on shoulders", which meant grasping the rifle with both hands, holding it horizontally, and pushing it straight up overhead, then back down to the shoulders- up, down, up, down, alternating between in front of the face and behind the head. While pushing his rifle up and down, the recruit shouted, "FIFTY THOUSAND MARINES WITH RIFLES, AND I'M ONLY A SHITHEAD WITH A GUN." After a minute or two, the rifle seemed to gain weight, as if it were made of lead. The physical training didn't bother Holloway. He was naturally athletic, having been the offensive tackle on the American Falls High School football team. He'd also done very well as an amateur boxer. His 5'8", 156-pound frame was composed of bone, sinew, and muscle. With almost thin legs, he had a broad chest tapering down to a 29" waist. His heavily muscled arms could do push-ups 'til the cows came home.

There were some things that Holloway had trouble getting used to. For one thing, he liked to eat. But the way chow was served apparently was to train the young men's taste buds for eating out of a mess gear in the field. Bacon, eggs, syrup, piled in a heap, and smothered with gravy. Food was never separated and always covered with gravy. Another thing that bothered him was the constant yelling at the young men as if they were disobedient dogs. But Holloway wasn't the only one bothered by that. During one scathing tirade, the D.I. challenged: "If anybody doesn't like this he can step out here right now!" Holloway saw some movement to his left and turned his head to see Harry Grambauer step out of the group. Harry had been one of the first people Holloway had met at the recruiting station. He liked him—a big Montana country boy with an easy-going manner, Harry had decided that he couldn't forego an opportunity to register his indignation. "Since you're asking, I've had about enough." Holloway couldn't remember who swung first, but Harry obviously knew how to use his fists and he could pack a punch. The D.I. got in some licks too, but by the time guards were able to subdue the young recruit, the older Marine had been soundly thrashed. Harry was hauled away to the brig. Holloway wouldn't see him again until he ran into him on a small Pacific island (Tulagi), and Grambauer would be giving haircuts to Marines.

On the third day the young men were separated into small units to accomplish some work details. Holloway's group was assigned to moving mattress pads from one area to another. It was easy. Actually, a pleasant change from marching and calisthenics with verbal accompaniment. They weren't working hard. The work was getting done and the young men enjoyed breaking a sweat in the southern California sunshine. Roll up the mattress pad, carry it over to the truck, where another Marine would stack it in the bed of the truck. If a Marine felt the need for a nature call all he had to do was walk across the street to the latrine. That's what Holloway was doing when he got into trouble again. He had crossed the street and was 20 feet from the latrine when he heard a very loud voice from across the street—"Hey you, come back here!" Holloway stopped and turned to face the origin of the offending voice. Standing there was a tall man in a clean light-colored shirt. The most noticeable thing about him was that he didn't have any stripes on his arm. He didn't have even one stripe anywhere on his clothing. Holloway had been taking a ration of shit from a pack of yahoos with stripes. They had taught him that if they had a stripe you were supposed to salute and take what they dished out. But Mr. Clean Shirt across the street was where he drew the line. No stripes, no salute, no shit accepted, thank you very much. His first response, when being yelled at, was to yell back. When in a situation that calls for quickly choosing a response it's quite often recommended to go with your first gut feeling. That's what Holloway did. He yelled back at him "If you want to talk with me, you come over here!"

If he hadn't been mad, Holloway might have laughed at Clean Shirt's reaction. His face had gone red and his eyes bulged in rage. However, the next exclamation bellowed from the man's mouth let Holloway know the seriousness of his mistake. "Guards! Throw that man in the brig!" Holloway had screwed up. As he would find out later, the other man was Lt. Colonel Groff, the Commanding Officer. He didn't suppose an apology would be accepted. No, it was too late for that. So the guards hustled him off to the brig. Round two went to the Marine Corps and Holloway was decidedly behind on points. But he was learning. From then on he would salute anyone in a clean shirt.

The brig consisted of six cells, each large enough to accommodate a cot and not much else. Bars separated those quarters from the guards. Two guards, on four-hour shifts, were on duty at all times to make sure the prisoners didn't try to escape. The guards were friendly enough, chit-chatting, asking what he'd done wrong. They did some chuckling when Holloway told how he had committed his faux pas. "Listen, Holloway, you had better learn some things right now. Tomorrow morning you'll be called in for office hours. That means you'll stand before the old man himself, you'll state your case, and he'll decide if and how you will be punished." The guards prepped him on how to stand at attention, click his heels, salute, and even what to say.

The next morning the prisoner was ready. He marched into the colonel's office, clicked his heels together, stood at attention, and saluted. "Private Holloway reporting for office hours, sir!" The CO was sitting at his desk, writing on some papers when Holloway entered the office. He hadn't looked up then and he still kept his attention on his papers. "Holloway, you have been charged with insolence, failing to salute an officer, and insubordination to an officer." He was still writing on the papers. "What do you have to say for yourself?" Holloway knew what he wanted to say in his defense. Just a few brief words. He opened his mouth... "Shaddup! Five days bread and water. Take him away!" He never did look up from his desk.

Your hair is cut short as soon as you are a Marine. When you go into the brig the hair is clipped right down to the scalp. Coming out of the brig, Holloway was thrown in with a brand new bunch of recruits and, with one glance at his cranium, they could tell he was a "brig rat." "Stay away from brig rats—they've been in trouble and nobody needs more trouble in boot camp." So Holloway had to live with the role of pariah for awhile. Nobody wanted to be around him or talk with him or even have eye contact with him. He was the invisible man and would remain that way until the nervous new recruits were relaxed enough to know he wasn't going to get their asses busted.

Back into marching, marching, and more marching. In the morning they were slapping their feet down in unison before the sun came up. Issued rifles, Springfield 1903s (called 03s), they added marching and saluting with rifles to their repertoire. Holloway was good at the marching. It wasn't uncommon to have the D.I. bellow "Platoon halt! What the hell's the matter with you guys? Can't you march in step? Holloway's the only one in step!" In their exhaustion at night the young Marines would still be marching even after their heads hit the pillow and deep slumber enveloped them.

On the firing range each recruit was tested as to how accurately he could shoot. They fired rifles from a standing position, sitting, prone—everything but firing over their shoulder using a mirror. They'd fire single shots as well as emptying out their rifles with rapid fire. Immediately after firing, they would be shown what pattern their shots had hit the target. If you missed the target completely a red flag would be waved. Any shots that missed the target were said to have gotten "Maggie's drawers." Holloway was given the grade of "Marksman" with a rifle, which was the lowest you could get. However, when tested with a pistol, he received the grade of "Sharpshooter." Right away he noticed the pistol was firing to the left, so Stan adjusted to the right and hit the human-figure target with regularity. Despite being tested on pistols, none of the enlisted men carried a pistol. Only officers had them.

As rigorous as boot camp was, very few of the recruits washed out. However, Stan's unit had one young man who was sent home after a few weeks because he couldn't read and memorize the written general orders and special orders, as was required. He was totally illiterate. Some of the others tried to help him memorize what he had to, but not being able to read was just too big a handicap. He had come out of the deep south, with no education. He wanted to fight for his country. He enjoyed marching and had no problem with the physical requirements, but he was finally sent home. From boot camp the

Marines went to Camp Elliott, located northeast of San Diego. The Marines stayed in big barn-like, two story buildings, with enough bunk-beds for about 30 guys per story. There the new Marines mixed in with veteran Marines, many who had seen duty at Iceland. Holloway liked the "old salts." They had a confident air about them and they were friendly. This dramatically changed the character of the outfit. No longer were they just a bunch of fresh kids. They were now teamed with veterans who knew the ropes, many having seen combat in China or Africa. One of the veteran Marines was a sergeant by the name of Benny White. He told stories about his travels all over the world, and he had commemorated his stays in foreign lands with tattoos all over his body.

In the early morning everyone would be awakened with a whistle. They would hurry to "fall out" and stand in formation, where there would be a daily roll call. At night "lights out" was at 10 o'clock, and bed checks were conducted with a flashlight. Unlike boot camp, where you were like a mouse on an exercise wheel, Camp Elliott allowed the Marines the luxury of getting to know each other. Holloway enjoyed talking with the others and making friends. One of them was Jerry Howery. Jerry was a farm boy from King City, Missouri. He liked to say that King City was "the Gem of the Highway and the Blue Grass Center of the World." Like Holloway, he was short and stocky, and used to hard work. The two young men were "birds of a feather." Howery was a talker, with the gift of gab and a sometimes-roguish wit. His playful sense of humor was occasionally regarded by others as needling. Jerry was used to people taking offense at his waggish witticisms, but that was okay. He could normally talk his way out of anything. Holloway never did see him pay for his humor with a butt kicking, but he did have to come to his defense a couple of times to save his teeth.

At Camp Elliott every Marine received his assignments. Holloway was in the 2nd Division, H & S Battery, 3rd Battalion, 10th Marines (Regiment). He was assigned to the Fire Direction Center of the H & S Battery, meaning that he was part of the artillery battalion that would fire "75 Pack Howitzers" at the enemy. His job was to survey in with

instruments on observation posts and enemy targets and to direct fire
at those enemy positions.

Maneuvers were conducted in the "Salton Sea", a large desert in
southern California. There they would fire the big howitzers at the
Chocolate Mountains. The H&S Battalion practiced calculating and
coordinating loft and direction of the big guns. With the other three
Batteries, each with four guns, they were able to land a lot of firepower
on a target. The Marines became familiar with the "75", the range, the
sound, the way the recoil would shake the ground. They took it very
seriously, practicing the deadly salvos on the Chocolate Mountains, so
that later they could use what they had learned to blast away at Japanese
encampments. As the war progressed the "75s" would be replaced by
"105s" (These were called "Long Toms", distinguished by a long barrel
and firing with a flat trajectory), and again by "155s." The "155s" had a
longer range and had much more arc in the trajectory. The Marines liked
to claim they could "lay it in a rain barrel at twelve miles."

While on maneuvers in the desert, the Marines became aware of the
dangerous creatures living there. There were plenty of rattlesnakes, with
a penchant for slithering into foxholes, which each Marine had dug next
to his pup tent. There was an army of scorpions that had them vastly
outnumbered and surrounded at all times. It seemed every rock or chip of
wood picked up had a scorpion under it. Add to that the centipedes,
which grew up to about 12" long and stung just like the scorpions.

These were some of the things to think about at night, sleeping in
a little pup tent. One morning Holloway awoke to the distinct feeling
that he was not alone—in the shirt that he'd worn to bed. Something
was moving around up near his shoulder. He was instantly wide awake,
and sweating in the early morning chill. There's nothing like the instant
threat of poisonous pain to fully wake a person. Pushing himself up
with the opposite arm, he carefully and very slowly lowered his arm,
and lightly shook the sleeve. He had to make sure he didn't pinch the
creature between the sleeve and arm. Holloway could feel it moving
down the sleeve toward his wrist. Very slowly the thing approached the
opening in the sleeve. Holloway could see the 10" centipede as it

lowered itself from the shirt to the ground. As he breathed a sigh of relief, a nervous shudder momentarily shook his body. When would they get out of this dangerous desert and into combat?

All the Marines had to put in their time on roving guard duty. On their four-hour shift they were strictly prohibited from doing anything that would either distract them or would give away their position, like eating, chewing gum, and especially smoking. They were checked on periodically by the corporal of the guard, who was checked on by the officer of the day. One night Holloway decided to take a chance and grab a quick smoke while on guard duty. He knew he shouldn't, but he really needed a cigarette, and they were just on maneuvers—nobody was going to shoot him. He lit up, and inhaled deeply. It was at about the third drag into the cigarette that he heard someone approaching. Cupping the butt in his hand, Holloway called out, "Who goes there?!" The officer of the day stepped out and identified himself. "I thought I saw a light out here." Closing his fist tightly on the burning butt, Holloway said, "I thought I saw a light also, sir." He tried not to wince as the ember seared into his palm and fingers. The officer glanced around, wondering where that light might have come from. "Carry on." He turned around and walked away. That was close—good thing the officer didn't detect the smell of burning flesh.

In between maneuvers the Marines were sometimes just kept busy. One day they were filling trucks with sand. The truck would back into a large sand hill where the men would shovel away, throwing the sand down to the truck. There were about 50 guys working away at a leisurely pace and it would take them about 10 minutes to fill a truck. As Holloway watched the next truck back up to the sand he remarked, "This is crazy. I'll betcha two men could fill that truck in fifteen minutes.

"I'll take that bet! And I'll bet a month's pay you can't do it!" The fellow who said it was not a favorite of Holloway's. His name was Stanford. Holloway knew him as a selfish loudmouth. Guys would get cookies from home and they would share with the others. Stanford would be first in line to get his goodies. But when he received a care package from home he would hide it. In the middle of the night they could hear him munching away, prompting some guys to get on his case: "What are you eating over there?!" Holloway would love to take a month's pay from Stanford but he wasn't sure it could be done. Maybe he had opened his mouth when he shouldn't have. "Stan, I'll be the other guy if you want to take that bet." A Texan by the name of Ward had offered to be the second shoveler. Holloway couldn't have picked a better guy for the job. Ward stood a little taller than Stan and had a lot of muscle. He was no stranger to hard work and had the stamina to go along with his strength. If anybody could hump for 15 minutes it would be Ward. Okay, there was no way to back out now.

The truck driver would signal when to begin and he would also signal when the load was full. The other Marines looked on as the driver backed his truck into the sand and Holloway and Ward took their positions and poised their shovels. "GO!" The two Marines started throwing furiously. They were like two madmen with shovels and the sand was flying. Holloway didn't watch the level of the sand in the truck. He was like a robot. His only thought was to shovel as fast as he could. After about 10 minutes he could feel the muscles in his back and arms tightening and he was huffing like a freight train. But he didn't slow down. And neither did Ward. The timekeeper called out the minutes and when it got to 14 everyone knew it was going to be very close. Finally, with about 20 seconds to spare, the truck driver signaled that he had a full load. The two men were worn out, but they had done it. Holloway's finances were looking pretty good. He let Stanford keep enough of his paycheck to cover his insurance, then he split the rest with Ward.

The Marines knew their Division, Regiment, and Battalion, but there were still more assignments and duties to be administered. The entire outfit was assembled by the colonel to appoint radiomen, electricians, painters, etc. The common joke was "If you were a blacksmith, the Marines would make you a cook." Sometimes the Marines would find your true calling. (For instance, a young man named Walter Hill was made a telephone man. On Guadalcanal Hill risked his life to run telephone line deep into Japanese territory and he received a commendation for it.) Working down the list, the colonel said, "Do we have any carpenters?" The silence that followed confirmed that there wasn't one trained carpenter in the whole outfit.

"I grew up on a farm. I can handle a hammer and nails." Jerry Howery stepped out from the group.

"You're now the battalion carpenter. But you'll need some help. Who else has had a hand at carpentry?"

Howery pointed at Holloway. "Stan grew up on a farm too. He could do it."

"Okay", said the colonel, "We have another battalion carpenter."

Holloway would be busy. Not only was he learning the business of artillery fire direction, but also now he was a battalion carpenter. That would include constructing 10-holers by the dozens, locker boxes, and officers' desks, among other things. In the field he and Howery would have to do some creative carpentry with whatever materials they could find.

Before shipping out to the Pacific, the Marines had to practice getting off a ship and onto a beach. These were called landing maneuvers. The first step was the hardest. It involved climbing down the side of the ship on a rope cargo net and jumping into a landing craft that was bobbing in the water like a cork. To miss-time the jump off the netting would mean a drop of about 10 feet. All of this was done with a rifle and a full pack, which weighed about 60 pounds. One of the Marines missed the boat when he dropped and landed in the water. In a matter of seconds he was squashed between the ship and the boat, like an insect being stepped on. It was a grisly lesson, but added emphasis for the other Marines to do the maneuver correctly. After practicing landings for a couple of weeks, they were ready. Ready to meet the enemy in the Pacific.

———

Chapter
TWO

The first ship the Marines would travel on was the *USS President Hayes,* a luxury liner that was being used for war duty. About 2,000 Marines would pile onto the vessel. Trying to make the ship look war-worthy and somewhat formidable, a five-inch gun was mounted on the fantail. Before the Marines were loaded on the ship they tested the gun. It was only fired once and the recoil caused so much damage that the former luxury liner had to be taken in for repairs. However, the big gun was left on the *Hayes,* just for looks. Finally, they were steaming across the Pacific. Accompanying the *Hayes* were the *Jackson* and the *Crescent City.* Also, nearby but out of sight were the carriers, the *Hornet* and the *Wasp.*

Holloway had always had a problem with motion sickness. A twenty-foot ride in the back seat of a car would have him "pitching his cookies." For a person like Holloway, an ocean voyage meant perpetual seasickness. It started when he left solid ground and remained a constant until he set foot again on terra firma. He felt as if he had drunk a bottle of turpentine and had been hung upside down. But the sickness wasn't totally debilitating. In fact, the Marine Corps did not regard sea sickness a reason for light duty—standing watch was still required. After a few days at sea, Holloway found that he could still function. So he volunteered for duty in the officers' mess. It wasn't bad—amounting to waiting tables in nice clean surroundings. He kept that duty for five weeks, until they reached their destination of Tulagi and Guadalcanal.

On the way they had two stops to make. At Fiji they would practice more landings. But first, they stopped at the Tonga Islands, and docked at a small harbor town on the island of Tongatapu. This is where Holloway, and many of the other Marines, saw Pacific natives for the first time. They were dark skinned with big fuzzy hair. The natives were also fascinated by the Marines. The command decided to give everyone a good look by marching the troops through town, turning them around, then back to the ship. The natives lined the street, excitedly running alongside the marching men, jumping up and down and waving. Never in all their lives had the young Marines seen so much nakedness. Most were wearing no clothing, and the rest had very little. The young men were marching on automatic, ogling the nudity like hungry coyotes at a sheep convention, and exchanging comments among themselves about the scenery.

That brief excursion was all they had time for because two Merchant Marine freighters had arrived to fuel the ships. Holloway volunteered to help with positioning the fuel hoses and, for that, he was invited to have lunch with the Merchant Marines. Their mess hall wasn't crowded, which was a nice change, and the food was better than what he had been eating. They sat there eating lunch, talking and joking around, and exchanging scuttlebutt. Holloway gained an immediate respect and admiration for the Merchant Marines. In order to keep the other ships running, they had sailed without an escort through dangerous waters, like fuel-laden sitting ducks. Besides, they were a nice bunch of guys.

After leaving the Tonga Islands and en route to the Solomon Islands, Holloway's ship was engulfed in a furious storm. Assigned to gun watch on the top deck, Holloway could hardly believe his eyes as the bow of the ship would dive into each giant wave, completely submerging the bow of the ship. At the end of Holloway's watch the officer of the day appeared and asked him to stay on duty for another four hours. There was no one to relieve him; everyone was too seasick. So he stayed on watch through another shift, and another after that. When he finally did make it below decks, he saw sick men lying everywhere. In the head, the toilets were designed with a stream of water running under the line of commodes. (It was a common joke to light something flammable and let it float down the water stream, burning butts all the way.) With the ship being thrown about, their toilet system was useless. There were men rolling around in the shit and vomit on the floor, puking uncontrollably. The sleeping quarters were the same way, with men throwing up everywhere and unable to stand up. Things remained that way for close to two days before the storm finally abated. Until that time, the other men had enjoyed ribbing Holloway about his seasickness. After the storm, there were no more comments.

The Solomon Islands consist of two parallel chains of islands with Guadalcanal being the largest at the end of the southern chain. About twenty miles north of Guadalcanal was the small island of Tulagi, with Gavutu, Macombo, and Florida nearby. Guadalcanal was an important piece of property because the Japanese were just finishing up an airstrip on the northern part of the island (later named Henderson Field by the U.S. after Major Lofton Henderson, who led the Marine dive-bombers at the battle of Midway). Whoever controlled that airstrip would have the advantage in the air war in the southern Pacific. To take Guadalcanal it was necessary to take the small islands near it as well, which were controlled by well-fortified, dug-in Japanese troops.

It was afternoon when the transport ship approached Tulagi. The Marines could see a few palm trees fluttering in the breeze, many with the tops knocked out of them by naval gun fire. Gazing at the tropical island, Holloway felt as if he were looking at a picture on a travel brochure for a beautiful vacation paradise. Then it hit them. The smell of the island. The smell of burning bodies. On top of being sea sick, Holloway felt the fetid stench seep into him. In combat you confront an enemy, but you find all of your senses being assaulted. But they didn't have time to dwell on the sickening smell. They had to be alert at battle stations. Practice was over. This was the real thing, and they had to be ready.

They saw the plane when it bounced over big Florida Island and headed for them. It was a Japanese Mitsubishi torpedo bomber, with designs on smashing a torpedo into the side of the transport ship. The plane's strategy was good. He dipped between them and a U.S. cruiser. Everything fired at the plane would be fired at the cruiser as well. The Marines had strapped 50 caliber machine guns to the railings all the way around. Their immediate survival rested entirely on those machine guns.

Holloway and another Marine were manning a water-cooled machine gun on that side of the ship. Holloway's job was to pump water through it as the other man fired at the plane. As he pumped as fast as he could, like pedaling a bike, only with his arms, he watched the plane come at them full throttle. They could barely hear the scream of the plane engine over the frantic chattering of the guns. Their bullets bounced off the cruiser like a deadly hailstorm. The plane rushed at them. Holloway could see the pilot; he could see the pilot's face. He could also see the machine gun tracers streaming into the plane. "What is holding him up?!" Holloway thought, "We're not going to stop him!" The men were yelling, cursing, commanding the plane to fall.

When it blew up, pieces of plane flew everywhere, some hitting the ship harmlessly, with the main part of the fuselage plunging into the ocean. The explosion indicated they must have hit the torpedo before it dropped. The pilot was probably dead well before that. An instant later there was an explosion of celebration from the men. The ship's captain announced over the speakers, "Every man on the port side of the ship will receive $5 reward for knocking down that plane." That was a good sized bonus; Holloway was being paid $21 a month, or as they liked to say, "$21 a day, once a month."

Now there was added urgency for getting the Marines off the transport ship. They couldn't risk other attacks with the ship packed full of men. So they hustled over the side, down the nets, and into the Higgins boats, which would take them into the harbor. The men were quiet, apprehensive. When the war broke out they thought it would be over quickly. But the Japanese had been planning for a long time and made preparations to be well manned and armed all over the Pacific Islands. The Marines had the feeling that this would be no cake walk.

It was approaching sunset and the shadows were lengthening. The island was quiet as they reached the dock. Holloway was manning the 50 caliber Lewis machine gun mounted on the back of the boat. He was nervous. Even though the Marine Raiders had landed in the first wave ahead of them, the Japanese still had a strong foothold on the island.

The "pop" of the sniper's rifle seemed to happen simultaneously with a whining "ping" sound as the bullet ricocheted off the edge of the boat. "There it is!" Holloway saw muzzle fire and a puff of smoke come from one of the trees. Quickly aiming at the spot, Holloway squeezed the trigger on the machine gun. The gun came to life, jumping with every blast of lead. Holloway could feel the powerful vibration surging through his arms and upper body. All of his concentration was centered on that target and all he could think was, "I'm going to get that sniper—he'll never shoot at us again!" He didn't know how many rounds he had fired, but when he stopped there was very little left of the top of the tree. Part of it cracked and fell to the ground.

"Jesus Christ, Holloway! Leave some for us!"

"You hate palm trees, Stan?!"

It was embarrassing. He looked down at the muzzle of the gun and it was glowing like a red-hot poker. The Lewis machine gun is air cooled and should be fired in short bursts. With the excitement of the moment he had forgotten that.

They stayed tied to the dock that first night. It wasn't exactly calm and peaceful because the Japanese talked to them from the high bluffs. "Hey, Mac. You're not going to live through this. You will die on this island." They kept extending such pleasantries for most of the night. Holloway had just drifted off to sleep when he was startled awake by yelling—close to him. "I can't take it! I can't take it!" One of the Marines was hysterical. "Let me go! I'll kill them! I'll kill them all!" The man had snapped. He would be put back on the ship at the first opportunity—get him out of there. They calmed him down and Holloway tried to go back to sleep.

At daylight they went ashore with little opposition and dug in. When the Marines established where they would camp, Holloway and his friend, Tom Enos, began building a shelter. They dug out an area, shoring the sides with rock and logs and covered it with more logs and sandbags from the beach. It was hard work and it took them several hours, but, when completed, it provided good protection.

One of the officers on Tulagi was Major Mills, a large man who walked and talked with obvious self-importance. His idea of leadership was to have the men fear him—and they did. No one wanted to be on the receiving end of his anger and, much to his consternation, Stan kept finding himself in that position. Major Mills became his nemesis.

The Major always needed something done for him. He would need his gear stenciled, or he would need to have a desk made for him. Whatever he wanted, he would look around for Holloway to do it for him. (He once made a desk for the Major on Tulagi with no nails and no other tools than a hatchet and a k-bar knife.) When addressing Holloway, he would pronounce his name by coughing out the first syllable and dragging out the rest of the name. It was a way he had of showing disdain for anyone he out-ranked. As the troops settled in, Major Mills walked around with his entourage, inspecting the camp.

"Whose shelter is this, HOLLowaayy?"

"That's mine and Tom Enos's, sir." He was proud of it. Maybe he'd be complimented.

"This will be our radio shack. Start hauling equipment in." "And, HOLLowaayy, do you see that log over there?" Major Mills pointed at a very large palm tree log.

"Yes, sir."

"I want you to place that log near the top of that hill", he pointed in another direction, "and I want you to make an officers' air raid shelter."

"But, sir, that is some of the heaviest wood in the world. That log must weigh a ton."

"Don't tell me your problems, HOLLowaayy. I don't care how you do it, just do it." End of discussion. Major Mills turned and walked away. Holloway did get it done, but it took the help of almost every man in the outfit to move that log. Invariably, after Stan would accomplish some Herculean feat, Major Mills would lambaste him with "See how easy it is—when you try, HOLLowaayy."

Holloway and some other Marines had made their way to the highest ridge on the island and were half-heartedly trying to dig foxholes in the rocky ground. It seemed like an exercise in futility trying to dig through the rocks with their small but tough collapsible shovels. Some of the men were just sitting around. One of them shouted, "Look, there's one of our cruisers!" Sure enough, sitting about a quarter of a mile out was a ship. The guys all stood up and excitedly waved, happy at having a cruiser there to support them. BOOM! They saw it before they heard it. One of the big guns on the ship had fired. The round sailed over their heads and landed with an explosion on Macombo Island, just behind them.

"God damn it! That's a Jap cruiser!" That blast had narrowly missed them. But it provided the motivation for digging foxholes. All of them had their butts in the air, furiously chipping away at the rocky terrain. The Japanese ship had sent a message that they could use the Marines for target practice any time they wanted. But being shot at wasn't what bothered the Marines the most. It was the sinking feeling in their guts of being abandoned. The Navy had sailed off and left them on their own. With the Navy had gone their supplies and both military and moral support. They would have to survive on their own.

The Japanese Navy could cruise around and do whatever they wanted with impunity. One night one of their cruisers turned a super-bright search light on them. They had been using it to search for a YP boat (a small maneuverable craft, commonly referred to as a "yippy" boat). They knew the Marines had one in the vicinity, but they didn't know where it was. (It was hidden in the harbor.) That little yippy boat could be a nuisance for them, so they wanted to get rid of it. The search light lit up the area as if it were daylight, making the hiding Marines feel exposed. One of the cooks thought the light was so bright the Japs wouldn't notice a cigarette, so he lit up. Immediately, the other men yelled at him "Put out that cigarette!" A stupid blunder like that could get them all killed.

With the Navy gone, their food supply was gone too. Luckily, they found an abandoned Japanese Supply House that was loaded with bags of rice. That would take care of what to eat—for a while. The rice was mealy, but the Marines didn't mind. In fact, as they got hungrier for nutrition they came to appreciate extra protein in their food. If something squirmy tried to crawl out of their rice they would scoop it back in and eat it. Also in the supply house were a few samurai swords and other collectibles, which were purloined by the first Marines there. Holloway grabbed a rectangular wooden box, about 18 inches long, that had twist chewing tobacco in it. That tobacco turned out to be valuable in bartering for other things. The natives loved it—in turn he always had his clothes well laundered.

The Marine Raiders had landed first and had done a major part of the fighting on Tulagi. It gradually became apparent that there would be no Japanese offensive. But the threat of snipers was still there. That's what Holloway was thinking about as he walked through the jungle to get to the spring for water. He had heard the one rifle shot up ahead of him. And now he saw a Marine walking toward him. As he got closer the other man said, "Watch out down there. A damn sniper almost got me." He took off his helmet and both of them looked at the holes near the top of it. The bullet had gone clear through, front to back, just missing the top of his head. Holloway was real edgy as he made his way to the spring. He was just starting back when he heard another gun shot. Shortly after that he heard some automatic weapons firing. Holloway cautiously walked back up the path, past where he had met the other Marine. Then he met him again. Only this time the Marine was sprawled on the path, dead. He'd been shot between the eyes. The automatic fire that he'd heard was some other Marines finally dispatching the sniper. The Japanese marksman had been hidden in a tree on a hillside with a good view of the trail. As he sighted down the trail he saw two Marine targets. He chose the one walking back from the spring and narrowly missed him on the first shot. Probably knowing he'd only have time for killing one of them, he again chose to shoot at the same Marine. His aim had been true on the second try. Jap snipers commonly tied themselves in trees, signifying their last stand. Holloway looked at him dangling upside down from the tree limb and wondered, "Why did he shoot the other Marine and not me?

Within about 10 days most of the men were stricken with malaria and dysentery. The sick men were so weak they couldn't stand up and certainly couldn't make their way to the latrine. At first, Holloway was one of the few still able-bodied. He kept busy helping Jerry Howery and Tom Enos, who were so debilitated they could hardly move. They suffered with a high fever, head and body aching, and a general malaise. The dysentery kept their bowels moving, so they were having to continually relieve themselves into their helmet and Holloway would carry their helmets to the latrine and dump them. (The steel helmet was their most valuable piece of equipment. They would bathe with it, boil water and cook in it, use it with its liner as a pillow, and it would protect the head pretty well.) With so many of the men sick, there just weren't enough to even take care of guard duty. Holloway had to cover his shift and stay on duty for those who were sick. No one escaped the sickness, and eventually Holloway was wracked with it too.

It didn't take long to take control of Tulagi. Most of the Japanese were killed. There were about ten prisoners who were kept in a large cage. One day some natives brought a Japanese prisoner into camp. His wrists and ankles were bound and the natives had run a pole through to carry him like a pig being carried to a luau. The prisoner grunted as his captors unceremoniously dumped him on the ground, but he didn't try to move around at all. Judging from the contusions on the visible parts of his body, it was obvious that the islanders had given him a severe beating. The natives hated the Japanese. They had suffered through all kinds of sadistic abuse, torture, and death at the hands of the Nipponese. When the Japanese lost their stranglehold on the islanders, they quite often found themselves on the receiving end of beatings or worse.

The Marines had been on Tulagi since early August. Then one day in mid-November reconnaissance planes came back with word that the Japanese were headed their way with 12 transport ships packed with thousands of soldiers. They expected them to arrive soon, probably that night, and the prognosis was not good. The Marines on Tulagi would be over-run. There was nowhere to go and no U.S. Navy to help them. All that could be done was to distribute the extra ammunition to the men.

Holloway and Tom Enos dug a foxhole together between two rocks, building it up with coconut logs and sandbags, and, finally, rocking it up around the edges. They had grabbed their share of extra ammo, including a full case of hand grenades. If they were over-run, they'd be tossing hand grenades to the end. Now all they had to do was wait. As they passed the time, they talked about how things had been back home. Tom told about how his parents had paid (what seemed like a fortune to Stan) for clarinet lessons. They had seen musical promise in him and, as a result, he had become an accomplished musician.

That night they listened to the radio. Two small PT boats were going out to meet the Japanese force and to radio back information. It was a suicide mission for the PT boats; they wouldn't last long against Japanese battleships. The radio crackled, "It looks like they're coming in. Get ready." The Marines hunkered down in their shelters and watched for the approaching enemy. Every nerve in their bodies was tingling. They knew death was approaching. This would be their last stand. That's when the PT boats heard the surprising announcement from the command of a battleship, "This is the *U.S.S. South Dakota*. Move aside." The *South Dakota* and the *Washington*, two powerful battleships, escorted by four destroyers, had shown up at the last possible moment to even out the battle. The Marines felt relief wash over them. They had been given a reprieve from certain death.

Sitting on a high bluff on Tulagi, in the middle of a dark night, they watched the battle at sea. As the U.S. battleships fired, the tracers trailed one after another, "like a string of wieners being pulled out of a sack" Holloway would later say. And when they hit something significant there was an explosion that would light up the sky. Just like a fireworks display. But the best thing was—it definitely looked like the U.S. battleships were winning. And win the battle they did. All the Japanese transports were disabled and sunk. The ones that weren't sunk were beached on Guadalcanal. It was a resounding defeat for the Japanese. The U.S. Navy was back in control.

Once the island was secure, Tulagi became a vacation resort for the Marines. Holloway got used to floating in the salt water for hours at a time. Beneath him he could see a multifarious collection of brightly colored fish slowly swimming around. The sun beat down on him, turning his skin a dark brown. Sometimes he would read a paperback novel as he floated on the water. If he needed a cigarette he'd paddle over to the dock, someone would give him a cig, light it up, and he'd continue his relaxed floating. He had found a piece of paradise, and he was still alive. No troubles with the war there. The marines spent so much time in the water that all the men had ear infections. At sick bay the medics would dip some cotton in Mercurochrome and stuff it in their ears. With most of the men walking around with cotton protruding from both ears, they came to be called "jungle bunnies."

When Holloway was on the job he was normally at the Fire Direction Center where radio contact was kept with the lookouts. Those outposts were located not only on Tulagi, but also on Florida Island and other close islands. The challenge for the Marines stationed out there was to deal with the monotony. Hours of watching for approaching enemy when they knew that if anything were to start to happen they'd get an advance warning from reconnaissance planes. Any break in the boredom was very much appreciated, so Holloway would sometimes try to liven things up. He had a talent for remembering and reciting poetry and toasts, and it came in handy sometimes to provide some entertainment. (He claimed he could continue making toasts as long as the beer held out.) The most appreciated poetry with the Marines was the off-color type like "The Grooving of Dan McGrew" or "Old Nell Brown" and Holloway was always being asked to "tell it again", especially by the guys on lookout. That's what he was doing over the radio one quiet night. He'd just finished the ballad of "Old Nell Brown" when a loud indignant voice blasted from the radio, "WHO SAID THAT?" An officer had heard the unauthorized chatter and decided to put a stop to it. No one answered him, but the men in the Fire Direction Center, and more than likely the outposts, were breaking up with laughter.

The Marines on Tulagi knew there were sea battles going on nearby even if they couldn't see them. Two U.S. cruisers limped in and navigated up a river on nearby Florida Island to undergo temporary repairs. One of them had the bow shot off and the other was missing the fantail. They were quickly patched up so they could make it to Hawaii for full repairs.

Meanwhile, the relaxing days on Tulagi were about to come to an end. About a dozen of the men, including Holloway and Jerry Howery, were shipped to nearby New Hebrides to do some training with Carlson's Raiders. The Raiders were an elite Marine Corps unit trained to do guerilla fighting behind enemy lines. From the crack of dawn to well past sundown, Holloway and the others ran through the drills. The Marines had to be in top shape, and Holloway and Howery certainly were. A main emphasis of the drills was on hand to hand combat. They learned how to kill a man close up. It had to be second nature. If attacked with a knife, grab the hand, quick twist, throw the man, bring the arm back between your legs and break the arm. Holloway found that he could fling a 200-pound man with ease.

At the end of the day the exhausted Marines would make it back to their shelters in the dark and crawl into their sacks for sleep. (There were no sleeping bags. They slept in canvas sacks with a blanket.) Each man had a shelter half, which would connect with snaps to another shelter half, in which both men would sleep. The sleeping arrangements would have been fine with Holloway, except that New Hebrides had spiders that favored sleeping in the shelters also. Holloway hated spiders. In fact, it could be said that he had a fear of spiders. But these were not ordinary arachnids. They were huge. After first arriving there, Holloway had watched in horror as a Marine dropped a helmet over one of the spiders—it's wiggling legs stuck out around the helmet. Luckily, they weren't poisonous and were not known to bite. But they could weave webs that were like little ropes. The first thing Holloway would do, when getting back to his sleeping shelter, was to feel for "ropes" blocking the entrance. After breaking them loose, he would have to feel around in the dark for the spiders, which he would then brush out of the shelter. Howery didn't seem to mind them as much. Holloway tried to mask his phobia by quietly grumbling as he searched for the awful things and Howery seemed to be having fun, giggling and gibing Holloway.

When the Marines returned to Tulagi they were told to get ready to leave again. They would be going to Guadalcanal, which was only 20 miles away, and they would traverse that distance in YP (yippy) boats. Holloway watched as the first boat made the journey across. They had almost made it when a Japanese cruiser, hidden behind Savo Island, started firing at them. They were getting hit dead center and the boat was going down. Not very many of the men would make it to shore.

A friend of Holloway's, Ike Iconelli, was on that yippy boat and he later told Stan about it. As soon as they had been hit Ike started throwing bodies and the wounded overboard. There was a mad scramble of Marines trying to get clear. Their only chance was to swim for shore. When Ike jumped into the water he saw a tin box floating nearby, so he grabbed it and started kicking for the beach. As he got close to shore an officer saw him and shouted, "Hey, Ike, don't lose that box—it's got the battalion payroll in it." After that fiasco, the Marine command decided to wait about a week before transporting the rest of the men over. This time, they would make sure there were no Japanese ships around to blow them out of the water.

They went in LSTs. When the landing craft got to the beach the front end dropped and they all ran up onto the beach. It was like a landing practice. There was heavy fighting going on elsewhere on the island, but not there.

The Marines set up their bivouac (camp) near the end of Henderson field. The big guns were positioned a short distance away. Holloway's mission was to help get the artillery firing at some targets, so he picked up his rifle and went out on his own. In order to determine the firing coordinates for the guns, he would venture miles from camp to a position where he could locate the enemy as well as a forward observation post. The entire island would have already been mapped out and divided up in grids with every hill and valley identified and numbered. When the forward observers saw a concentration of enemy they would call the Fire Direction Center (FDC) to report it. An officer there would announce, "Fire mission!" to alert everyone at FDC. Then it was Holloway's job to pinpoint that location on the map. Using a scope device on a tripod called an "aiming circle", he would survey in the target. Holloway would have to get used to these solitary missions. When the artillery was set up and needed a target, he would have to be out there. In this case, they were blasting the Japanese strongholds from a distance of about five miles.

The Japanese also had artillery, known as "Jap 77s", big guns that fired shells about eight inches in diameter. By the time Holloway made it back to camp the Japanese had directed their artillery at the Marines. The first warning the Marines had that the 77s were firing on them was the whishing sound, like air escaping from a spinning tire, announcing the shells were coming at them. As the men dove into their slit trenches, the first shells exploded in the middle of the camp. The Japanese had zeroed in on their encampment. WHISH, WHISH, WHISH, WHISH, BOOM. Holloway tried to sink as far as he could into the mud as the 77s delivered the deadly bombs in rapid succession. Some of the shells were duds that would hit with such velocity that the earth would shake as they bounced through the camp. .

When the barrage ended Holloway lifted himself out of the trench and sat there peeling the mud off his face with his fingers. He could see some other men starting to move around. Despite the ringing in his ears, there seemed to be a momentary silence. Holloway turned his head to the right and felt a sudden tightness in his guts as he reached out his arm and laid his hand on a 77 dud. It was less than 3 feet from him.

Despite being somewhat removed from front line rifle fire, the men still had to continually watch out for Japanese planes, called "Zeros." They could drop out of the sky at any time and cut you to shreds. For some reason, Holloway was able to hear planes approaching long before anyone else could. In fact, his acute hearing could generally tell whether or not it was a Zero. If it were, he'd start yelling for everyone to take cover.

One night as Holloway lay on his cot under the mosquito netting, he was awakened from a light, ready-to-jump sleep. He could hear a plane in the distance. The high-pitched engine whine sure did sound like a Zero. "Zero coming in! Take cover!" he yelled, and could hear some of his comrades groan and complain as they took heed. Every man had dug a slit trench next to his cot. For quick protection all he needed to do was roll off the cot and into the trench. The only problem was it rained a lot and that made the slit trenches prime spots to make mud pies, but not to lie in. Lying in the mud, the wet and the cold would bring out the shivers. Add to that the impending probability of machine gun fire and flying shrapnel. Now they could all hear it. The plane dipped over the hills, cruised in, and landed on Henderson Field. It was one of ours, a PBY.

"Dammit! That's a PBY, not a Zero, Holloway!"

"Thank you, Holloway, you S.O.B!"

What could he say? Holloway pulled on some dry clothes, wrapped a Marine Corps blanket around him, and tried to get back to sleep. He'd been asleep for about four hours when something started pulling at his dream consciousness, beckoning him to wake up. He had learned not to ignore such intrusions. As Holloway floated back into reality he became aware of the musty smell of the hot-wet jungle and he could hear snoring from nearby Marines. There was something else he could hear. Very faintly—"prrrinng, prrrinng, prrrinng", the sound of a Jap Zero. He had to be sure. Two false alarms in one night and he'd might as well camp out on the other side of the island. The closer it got the more it sounded like a Zero. Then it cut the engine off. That was it! It had to be a Zero! The pilot had cut the engine to glide over without being heard. "Jap Zero! Jap Zero! Get under cover!" Holloway shouted, as he hustled around trying to alert everyone. But they weren't going to listen to him this time. "Holloway, you S.O.B., it's probably one of ours!" Guys were grumbling and throwing stuff at him. The Zero silently glided over the airstrip. Then the pilot turned it around, fired up the engine, and started dropping "daisy cutters", little bombs that would throw shrapnel everywhere. This was no false alarm. Marines dove for cover wherever they could. Holloway ran for a little air raid shelter they had made. The opening he scrambled for had a fat guy crawling into it. With the daisy cutters getting closer, the fat guy wasn't fast enough for Holloway. So he jumped on the guy's back and rode him in, as the top of the entrance scraped the hide off his back.

When things settled down and Holloway came out of the shelter, he could hear someone screaming. It was a guy who had been in the latrine when the Zero cut loose on them. He had been out in the open and couldn't find protection. The guy was lucky the daisy cutters didn't leave him in several pieces. But he was a casualty anyway. Holloway could see him running around, yelling and crying. Every once in a while falling to the ground, then getting up, looking for protection that would never be there. He had been blasted into craziness. Holloway recognized him; he knew him. He was a young man who believed in the Bible, and who liked to talk about his Christian faith. He and Holloway had had several conversations. The guy had been friendly, a nice kid. Now he was a blubbering madman. Holloway ran after him, as did some others, and held him still while trying to calm the young man down and bring him back to reality. "It's okay. It's okay. The plane's gone. You're safe now." But his mind was shattered, his face contorted, and his eyes unfocused, as he lay on his back and struggled against his friends holding him down. He screamed and cried until the medics injected a strong sedative to knock him out.

From then on, when Holloway said an enemy plane was coming in, everybody jumped. If the Zeros came looking for trouble during the day, U.S. planes, Wildcats, would take off to meet them and the Marines would watch the dogfights. They were quite evenly matched, with the Zero's quickness and the Wildcat's superior armor. Then the U.S. brought in four P-38s that were much more powerful than the Zero. They would fly straight up under a group of Zeros, knock some of them down on the way through, and then fly back down at the hapless Zeros. The Marines would cheer them on. As the P-38s took control of the skies over Guadalcanal, the Japanese pilots made fewer and fewer strafing runs.

Thanksgiving Day of 1942 found the Marines taking a short break to enjoy the turkey dinner that had been shipped in for them. The weather was sunny and warm. Holloway was sitting on a log, a full plate on his lap, thoroughly enjoying every morsel. Around him, he could hear the men joking with each other, reminiscing a little bit, or maybe grumbling about something. That's when a jeep pulled up with a lieutenant behind the wheel. "Come on, Holloway; we've got a mission." Thanksgiving dinner was abruptly over. It was back to work.

They drove across the terrain without saying anything to each other and began to ascend one of the small ranges on the island. Holloway knew better than to question the officer—he would know soon enough what he had to do. About a quarter mile from the ridge the lieutenant stopped the jeep. That was as far as he would go. Holloway, however, was to continue to the top and, from there, figure the distance and range to drop some artillery fire on the enemy. As he moved quickly through the brush, all Holloway could think about was the food that he'd left behind. His palate remembered that last hurried spoonful of dressing and gravy. It was Thanksgiving Day and he was hungry.

From the top of the ridge, Holloway could see clear across the island. Using the aiming circle and his map, he spotted the location of enemy trucks and troops that the forward observer had called in. To the left Holloway could see a large white rock in the distance. From his map, he knew exactly how far away that rock was. Using that as a focal point, he could discern the exact distance and deflection of the enemy position. All he had to do was take the readings and write them down. There was only one complicating factor. The enemy was firing at him. Holloway heard the sharp pops of rounds hitting the dirt near him. He couldn't see the Japanese soldiers in the brush below but they could obviously see him. The firing rapidly got heavier and he tried to keep his hands steady as he noted the final coordinates. Time to go. He grabbed the legs on the aiming circle and collapsed them as he ran for cover. A couple of rounds sailed past his head as he crouched low and scrambled back to relative safety behind the ridge. Then he quickly made his descent to the waiting jeep.

That night a runner was sent to fetch Holloway. He woke him up with, "Say, Holloway, you're in trouble! Grivitch ran your figures on the map and where you set up wasn't right. You were way off target." It was a big mistake. The aiming circle had not been declinated for magnetic north, or adjusted for their position on that island. Someone had neglected to do that. Of course, when the coordinates were put down on a map, Sgt. Grivitch noticed right away that something was wrong. For that screw-up Holloway was assigned mess duty, which was fine with him. The Staff Sergeant in charge of the mess was a friend of his.

When the Army arrived at Guadalcanal the Marines were happy to see them. Their joy centered on what the army had brought with them—candy bars and cigarettes. It was cause for celebration to be able to walk down to the Army PX and buy some candy bars. Holloway knew that the Marines would probably be leaving soon and he didn't want to run out

"The Marines huddle on the bottom of the boat all ready to jump ashore as soon as the ramp is dropped."

Guadalcanal, McElroy

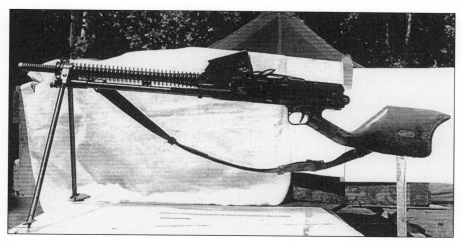

"Jap Nambu, hopper fed light machine gun. Guadalcanal 2/19/43"

Mar.Gun. J.F. Leopold, 2nd Mar.Div.

of cigarettes wherever they were going, so he went down to the Army PX and bought 10 cartons. That should last a while. But Guadalcanal was a wet, rainy, muddy, humid island and within a week the cigarettes started to mold. They were a total loss—he couldn't give them away. All the others had bought cigarettes too, and they were all ruined.

By early January, 1943, there were about 50,000 American troops on Guadalcanal, including 14,733 Marines from the 2nd Division, pushing the estimated 25,000 weary Japanese across the island. The American dominance of the air stifled the Japanese attempts to reinforce their troops. Henderson Field became fully operational and was an important factor in the taking of Guadalcanal, establishing U.S. air superiority.

As the Japanese fell back toward Cape Esperance, aerial reconnaissance alerted U.S. commanders to a large naval buildup at Rabaul, and it was thought they would attempt to re-take Guadalcanal. However, the Japanese had decided to concede the island to the U.S. They evacuated the remainder of their troops onto awaiting ships and sailed away. Amazingly, their evacuation went undetected by American generals. They just disappeared from the island. Guadalcanal would be the longest battle of the war for the Marines. Total American ground forces lost in combat were 1,598 killed and 4,709 wounded, of which the Marines had 1,152 dead and 2,799 wounded. Marine aviation units also had 55 killed, 85 missing, and 127 wounded.

Finally, with the Japanese pushed off the island, the Marines were able to relax a little bit. Holloway and Jerry Howery would explore parts of the island—they called it "souvenir hunting." As they traipsed through one partially cleared area, Howery stopped, looked around him, and excitedly shouted "Goobers!" As Howery knelt down, running his fingers through the low-lying plants, Holloway stood there baffled.

"What is it, Howery?"

"Stan, we raise these back home. These are goobers—peanuts!" He was laughing. "And it looks like a decent crop."

They didn't waste any time. Digging up as much as they could carry, they made it back to camp and gave some to the cook. He happily made the peanuts part of the next meal. The rest they ate for snacks, sharing with the others. The "goobers" were a big hit. In fact, too much so. Within a couple of days the peanut patch had been picked clean and the plants were decimated. It looked like a herd of wild Marines had stomped through it.

One event that was sure to evoke excitement was the arrival of mail. Sometimes the mail wouldn't catch up to them for several months, but when it did the occasion was just like Christmas. Mail call would become a frenzy of enthusiasm. The Marines would read and re-read the letters, hearing the voices of those they loved, telling them the news of their cherished home. Holloway loved getting letters. Normally he would receive news from Mom, Aunt Mildred, cousin Ruth, and a friend named Helen. They would ask him, "Is there anything we can send you?" and he asked them to send cigarettes. Mail call and Stan's cigarettes arrived right after the army appeared on Guadalcanal, and, of course, those cigarettes rotted away.

It was, once again, time for the men to move on to parts unknown. They boarded the transport ship not having the foggiest idea where they would end up. It was seasick time for Holloway. He knew he'd be sick as long as he was aboard ship, so he volunteered for work in the laundry, a place that seemed to make others sick. So what would be the difference—he felt like he was turned inside out anyway. The laundry area was clean and turned out to be a decent place to have duty.

"Japanese light machine gun calibre 25. Guadalcanal, Feb. 19, 1943"

-Sgt. J.H. Sutton, 2nd Mar. Div.

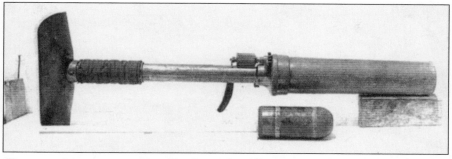

"Japanese knee mortar (grenade thrower) with grenade. This weapon is spring actuated. Guadalcanal, 2/19/43"

-Sgt.J.H Sutton, 2nd Mar. Div.

"Stripped for action: The Marine crew of this 155mm Howitzer prepares for action against the Japanese on Guadalcanal during the Solomon Islands campaign. The artilleryman in the left foreground prepares a powder charge while others adjust sights and fix the gun trail into position. 2/9/43"

"Jap heavy machine gun with clips. Guadalcanal 2/19/43"

Sgt. J.H. Sutton, 2nd Mar. Div.

"'Pistol Pete' the Japanese 108 mm. rifle. Guadalcanal 2/19/43"

Sgt. J.H. Sutton, 2nd Mar. Div.

PACIFIC WAR MARINE

Chapter
THREE

———

*T*he weekend in Pullman had been productive, talking with Dad and getting more information. I would be leaving that day, Monday, but first I would have lunch with my parents at the senior center.

We drove across town in their car, with Mom driving. Dad, of course, insisted that I sit in the front—I quite often will argue the point, but not that day. It used to be that Dad couldn't ride in the back seat without getting ill, but as he got older something changed and he no longer gets sick.

As we walked across the parking garage in the courthouse basement, our pace was slow—we were in no hurry. Mom is a fast walker, she keeps fit playing tennis. But Dad has slowed down. He no longer takes walks every day. His exercise is limited to taking care of the lawn and the garden and, when the snow falls, he gets out the snow blower and clears snow for himself and the neighbors. For any harder projects the next door neighbor, Bob, and his wife, Leslie, are in constant touch and Bob is always helping Dad with something. The last few years have given Dad's posture the look of someone bent at the waist, beach combing, which he loves to do.

On the elevator to the second floor Dad said, "Son, Momma and I have really enjoyed having you here." Mom added, "Don't forget to take some raspberry jam with you."

We were early as we entered the cafeteria room reserved for the seniors' lunches. Mom took her position at a table near the door to greet people and collect money as Dad and I got some coffee and seated ourselves at one of the tables. The room filled up with elderly folk—the final count would be between

39

40 and 50. Many had walkers, some were in wheelchairs. As they would have back in school, the seniors tend to sit with the same friends every time. At our table were several people who play bridge with Dad, mostly women. Talking with each briefly, I was warmed by their pleasant cordiality. Hearing aids were prevalent, but they can't seem to make up for the hearing loss. Even with them, words and phrases, even whole conversations can be lost.

We got our food cafeteria-style then took our seats. When everyone was seated, someone at the podium announced over the speaker system, "We will now do the pledge of allegiance." I stood and we began, "I pledge allegiance..." Looking around, I realized I was the only person standing. Others had pushed their chairs back to rise, but when you are 80+ years old it can be a slow process. By "One nation under God..." many were still struggling. Some didn't make it by "And justice for all."

We were just seated again when, "Now, for some announcements." The little lady across the table from me, thinking that since she couldn't hear the announcements, she might as well be talking and began to tell me a humorous story how her cat had learned to play the piano. Not Beethoven—just some miscellaneous notes. I looked around—everyone was talking. The announcements were lost in a sea of chatter. I looked at Dad. With a trace of a smile, he slowly shook his head. Afterward, during clean-up, I was talking to Diane Yettick with the Council on Aging. I had met Diane before at a senior lunch and she had told me about a project of hers. Diane was arranging interviews of local World War II veterans by high school students, and was putting them together in a book.[1] When I asked her how the project was going she said the book was almost completed. However, she hadn't been able to arrange an interview with Dad. He was very reluctant to take part in something that might have him speaking to a group.

Walking to the car, Mom and I asked Dad why he was so reticent to take part. He recalled a few years ago when he had been in an interview in front of 20-30 students and several veterans talked. The two other World War II vets had taken up most of the time "yakking away." I asked him about

[1] The book, entitled Tribute and published by Cougar Graphics in Colfax, Washington, contains the stories of men and women from Whitman County who were involved with World War II.

those other vets but he didn't remember very much about them except "They sure weren't Marines."

Later that day, Mom and Dad had Diane come over to conduct the interview and it went very well. They had a delightful chat over tea.

The rain pattered on the windshield as I drove down the Columbia River gorge toward Vancouver. I thought about what Dad had told me that weekend. Occasionally he would ask mom to clarify or add to the memories of New Zealand. He would call from the dining table, where we were seated, across the living room, where Mom was sitting, reading a book, "Momma, how far is it from Wellington to Paekakariki?" Mom would look up from her book and reply, "That's about 40 miles." They both told of how New Zealand had been left without any young men to help defend the country against the Japanese. Laughably, they had one antique gun at Fort Dorset, overlooking Wellington harbor. At other gun placements they had made wooden guns to look like the real thing.

In the midst of war there had been some happy times, and Dad was smiling and exuberant when telling me about them. But on the horizon were battles so ghastly that not even Tulagi and Guadalcanal could have prepared the Marines for them. Dad was serious when telling about the fighting and his eyes filled with tears as he remembered the pain and death. But some memories were too ugly to bring back. Much of the killing and suffering and atrocities that Dad saw will never be dredged up and will remain buried.

Normally the Marines were kept in the dark about almost everything. Rumors and speculation became the primary source of information. This communication was called "scuttlebutt", and it carried information through the ranks as fast as wildfire. Some of the info would turn out to be true, and every soldier had to determine how much of what he heard was worth passing on. As they plied through the Pacific waters, the scuttlebutt was that they were headed for New Zealand to rest until the next push.

The only thing Holloway and the rest of the men knew about New Zealand was that they had received rations from there. Those rations were the strangest they had ever seen—canned tongue, lamb, and other unknown foods. The Marines were anxious to see what kind of savages would inhabit the island and would eat that kind of food.

As soon as they pulled into Wellington Harbor, it was announced that they were in New Zealand. Then came another announcement. "Liberty will be granted to those with a clean shirt and a clean field scarf." Who had a clean shirt? Nobody! And a clean field scarf? Not a chance. Marines were frantically scrubbing shirts in the sinks. Others were ripping strips of canvas off shelter halves (half tents), trying to make field scarves. But Holloway was lucky. He was working in the laundry, a place where those things could be had. He would simply purloin a couple of officers' shirts and field scarves.

Wellington had the most beautiful harbor Holloway had ever seen. And on the hills surrounding the harbor was a modern looking city. He had a good feeling about this place. Holloway and Howery had big smiles on their faces as they marched off the ship and toward the welcoming sights and sounds of Wellington. They were the only two enlisted men to leave the ship.

From the dock, it was about a 100-yard walk up Willis Street to the heart of Wellington. There Holloway and Howery walked into a dance club. As they climbed the broad wooden stairs to the next floor their Marine Corps shoes clapped on the steps and echoed in the hallway. At the same time they could hear the small band in the large room ahead, belting out a popular dance song. The room was well lit. Not at all crowded, the room was filled mostly with young women, and a few men. Some were dancing, while others were talking and laughing at the edges of the room. There were chairs all the way around.

This was one of several dance clubs in Wellington. Girls signed up and joined these clubs to lend a hand to the war effort. New Zealand had been at war for two years now and everyone had a vested interest in the war. They could only imagine the horror of what it would be like if the Japanese stormed onto their islands and took control. These young girls were determined that the visiting young Marines would feel welcome and happy. One of the primary rules of the clubs was that the girls were not to ever refuse a dance. This fit into the Marines' plans perfectly. They could dance as much as they wanted—and the girls were so friendly! When the band would take a break, everyone would descend the stairs to the ground floor and help themselves to the hors d'oeuvres, small sandwiches, and tea that was spread out on tables for them.

The Marines danced and played the night away. As Holloway and Howery walked down Willis Street toward their ship, they laughed and joked with each other. It felt good to be so relaxed.

The next day the Marines traveled north from Wellington about 40 miles to the township of Paekakariki to set up their Divisional Camp. One of the first things Holloway did there was pull out a little electric iron that he'd brought with him. Announcing that he'd iron a shirt for 25 cents, he had guys lining up. He quickly smoothed out a couple of shirts. Business was clicking. Praise be to the free enterprise market! Holloway was going to make some money—then the iron quit. What the hell?! With a little investigating, Holloway found that N.Z. wiring was 220 volts, which would burn up a 110-volt iron. Another entrepreneur out of business. And he hadn't bothered to take care of his wrinkled shirts first.

The Marines found themselves with a lot of time on their hands and not a lot of activities around the camp. So they would converge on the local pub, which happened to be the only one in the area. For those with liberty, all one had to do was walk out the camp's main gate, march around the corner, and enter the pub. If you didn't have liberty you would crawl under an isolated part of the fence, sneak over a small ridge, walk onto the street and enter the pub. The place was always full of Marines.[2]

After about a week at Paekakariki, the 10th Marines moved 30 miles south to set up the artillery camp at Pauatahanui, which was 2

[2] Fifty years later Stan visited this pub. When the proprietor found out that he had been a Marine stationed there he said, "You're not paying for anything here."

miles from the town of Plimmerton. It was a lovely countryside, with scattered timber, farmlands, and sheep. Holloway was reminded of his rural roots as he inhaled the country air. When liberty came up he knew he'd be spending his time basking in the country life.

Pauatahanui had four-man huts for the men—they seemed very roomy and were comfortable living quarters. But there was a shortage of warehouses, which had to be built. For the construction of one very large warehouse, a group of New Zealand men were contracted to do the work and, as battalion carpenter, Holloway was assigned to assist the "kiwis." They were men past fighting age, but they were doing their duty at home. Holloway could see that they were skillful. He genuinely enjoyed working alongside them. They worked hard and the job went fast. It was this group of kiwis that introduced Holloway to the relaxing enjoyment of "tea time." Twice a day it would be time to "boil the billy." They would take a break and have a cup of tea. Holloway developed a taste for tea that would always be with him.

Another project Holloway worked on was making a "range table" for Colonel Curry. When finished, the 15' x 15' table was covered with green netting and imitated natural terrain, complete with hills, mountains, valleys, etc. The officers used the range table to simulate the challenges affecting artillery.

Besides carpentry work, Holloway was kept busy assisting the Property Sergeant. He'd been promoted from Pfc. to Corporal, but in that capacity his title was "Assistant Property Sergeant." The duties involved being responsible for the equipment belonging to the entire battery, including clothes, tools, and other things. When the battery needed equipment or supplies either Holloway or the Property Sergeant would go to the Quartermaster Section to obtain them.

Nearly every day would find Holloway going to the Quartermaster to draw supplies. He knew the handful of men assigned there, including Lieutenant Stein, who was in charge. On one of his short sojourns to pick up supplies Holloway asked permission to use the field telephone to call back to the property tent. When he tried to use the phone it was dead. Lieutenant Stein said, "Oh! I should have told you. Our electricity has been out now for a couple of hours."

"I don't think that would affect it, sir," said Holloway. "The field phones are battery operated."

"Are you trying to argue with me, Holloway?!"

"No, sir." Holloway had been taught early in life to never argue with a fool. He might as well try to explain astronomy to a dog.

A couple of days later Holloway walked into the Quartermaster for more supplies. As he entered the tent he could see the usual bunch of guys. However, Lieutenant Stein seemed to be absent. As he walked up to them, Holloway vociferously announced, "Hello boys! Is Stupid around?" Holloway imagined that they might see some humor in his remark. But he wasn't prepared for the loud guffawing laughter. There must be something else. He turned around and right behind him was Lt. Stein, who said, "Now, what did you do, Holloway? Tell a nasty story?" A wave of relief washed over Holloway. But he had started something. Lieutenant Stein would, from then on, be known as "Stupid" Stein.

In order to keep the men fit, the Marine Corps would, among other things, have them go on long marches with full packs. Holloway was preparing for one such march, stuffing his gear into a pack, when Martin, a big, surly 200-pound guy, decided to razz him. Martin didn't have to go on this march and he was the sort of person who enjoyed rubbing that in. Standing there watching Holloway roll up his gear, he casually kicked his boot against Stan's pack. Holloway asked him not to do that. He reached out again and kicked it over. Holloway up-righted his pack, looked at Martin, and said, "Don't do that again." Martin's boot kicked out again and, before the pack could topple over, Holloway had launched himself into his antagonist and had him down on the floor. Martin struggled to get away and to fight back, but Holloway was well on the way to giving him the full tour of the floor of the property tent complete with punches to the head and body. It took a handful of men to separate them. Martin never again tried to harass him. Fighting among the men was a common occurrence. When in combat situations, everyone was a brother. Holloway loved and cared about those Marines around him, and he knew they would do anything and everything to protect each other. However, resting between battles could be a different dynamic. These were energetic young men, filled with testosterone and a need for fun and excitement. The Marine Corps had trained and drilled them into fighting machines, in the best physical shape of their lives. With the addition of lots of alcohol, there could be a collision of tempers, pride and machoism. Sometimes the Marine Corps would bring in a large amount of beer, set it up in a tent, and sell it at very low prices. This was called a "slop shoot." The Marines would flock to the slop shoot, get drunk, and often end up in a fight. Upon returning to the states, many of the young men would first see a dentist to get their front teeth fixed.

Every outfit seemed to have at least one renegade. One man who didn't care about anyone but himself, and would cause trouble for everyone. In Holloway's battery that was Galbrist. He was a loudmouthed little guy who had an opinion or scathing remark to say about everything and everyone. Galbrist had been in Holloway's tent in Camp Elliot. When they caught him stealing, they opened up his locker box and found that he had lifted things from every man in the tent. When their battalion left the States, Galbrist was left behind, in the brig. He was awaiting trial to be court-martialed for stealing. Somehow, he talked his way out of it, and when replacements were sent in on Guadalcanal, there was Galbrist. Back with them again. When he showed up the men who knew him just groaned in disbelief, "He's back!"

In New Zealand Galbrist was spending time in familiar surroundings—the brig. Brig rats were used for clean-up detail—to pick up trash around the camp. To guard them, Marines had to follow them around (they called it "chasing prisoners") and make sure they didn't escape. The guards were inclined to watch them very closely for, if there was an escape, the Marine guarding that person would have to serve his sentence. One particular day, Holloway was assigned to watch Galbrist as he picked up trash. Galbrist asked him "What would you do, Stan, if I'd just take off here?" Holloway's reply was "You just take off and I'll show you." Galbrist looked at Holloway's rifle and decided not to press it.

In the brig with Galbrist was another hell-raiser named Frank Murphy. When Murphy would get drunk he would get obnoxious and would do his best to get into a fight. As a result, he'd sometimes end up behind bars. Holloway was one of the few men willing to tolerate being around him on liberty. One time on Guadalcanal, away from the front lines, Murphy and some other Marines were standing around drinking some alcohol made from raisins and called "raisin jack", feeling a bit tipsy, and bragging about past fights, when a young man named VanAble said "Well, I haven't been knocked down yet." Around Murphy, a statement like that was like waving a red flag in front of a fighting bull. Without warning, he hit VanAble as hard as he could right in the face. The punch shattered cartilage and mashed the kid's nose onto the side of his face. Holloway saw VanAble at chow the next day. His nose was a smashed mess. The kid got his food and dejectedly sat by himself, away from the others. So Holloway sat with him and tried to console the young man. He felt pretty bad. As the result of one impetuous moment, VanAble would have Murphy's handiwork left on his face for the rest of his life.

Holloway happened to be on guard duty when both Galbrist and Murphy were serving time. The prisoners were lounging around wishing the time to pass by quickly and, as usual, Galbrist was talking away—whining, complaining, etc. Holloway tried to tune him out. It could be a long four hours of guard duty with that continual yakking. Apparently Murphy felt the same way, or maybe he didn't feel like being drawn into any stimulating repartee. Holloway heard him loudly say "Shaddup!" Galbrist certainly heard Murphy's suggestion, but he chose to ignore it and plowed on with his incessant chatter. CLONK! It was the sound of a hard blunt object hitting skull bone. The Marines had just been issued new boots, each having a horseshoe-shaped steel attachment tacked onto the heel to slow down wear. Murphy had used one of his new boots to hammer Galbrist on the top of his head. Galbrist was out cold and would be sleeping for awhile.

That wasn't the only time that Galbrist was on the receiving end of a brain concussion. Late one night Holloway heard someone come into the property tent where he slept, and whisper "Hey, Stan." "Yeah." He'd learned to be a light sleeper. Barely opening his eyes, and trying to adjust his vision, Holloway saw his friend, Earl Lance, leaning down next to the cot. Earl's face looked ashen.

"I think I've killed that damn Galbrist."

"Good."

"No, I mean it." The two had had an argument, which developed into a fight. Earl had swung a tent pole at Galbrist and connected with the side of his head. Galbrist had dropped like a sack of potatoes.

When the two men got to the area of the fight, there was no Galbrist to be found. Apparently, he had come to and wandered off. Earl was very relieved. Later on Holloway would look back on that night and wish that Earl had killed Galbrist.

The idea of liberty is to get away from camp—to relax, have fun, and do what you like to do. For a short liberty, Holloway would walk down the road to the nearest neighbors, an older couple who lived on a small farm with their grandsons, ages 10 and 12. Holloway got used to relaxing and talking with the country folks. He would also help them with things like doing chores, cleaning the barn, or putting hay down for the livestock.

For a weekend liberty, Holloway would jump on a train and ride it north to the town of Otaki. The freight train would stop at the Plimmerton station and he would jump aboard. After a few trips the train people got to know him; they'd recognize him standing on the platform and he'd be invited to ride up front with the engineer. On the trip back the engineer would quite often just slow the train down without stopping so Holloway could step onto the platform. When he reached the Otaki station he had a one-mile walk to the center of town, and one more mile to the beach.

It didn't matter where you went in New Zealand, people were always inviting you in to eat, or to spend the night. That's how Holloway became acquainted with Charlie (Robbie) and Elsie Robertson. He met them on the street in the town of Otaki, they started talking, and he was invited for supper and lodging. He took an instant liking to them and they let him know that any time he could get liberty he was welcome there.

One night while Stan was having dinner with the Robertsons, Robbie mentioned that he had a fairly new car parked in the garage—a Morris 8. However, because of the stringent gas rationing, he hardly ever drove it. After supper, they went to the garage to look at the car. Holloway was thinking, "A Morris 8, with eight cylinders—with a large engine like that, it must be about the size of a big Buick." Then Robbie opened the garage doors and, sitting in the middle of the garage, was a tiny little auto. Holloway could have jumped over it. He walked around it, knowing that the bright, shiny, diminutive car could not possibly house eight cylinders. In fact, the "8" referred to 8 horsepower. As Stan would say later, "Those were eight powerful horses, not little ponies like what you find in cars today."

With gasoline in its tank, that cute little automobile would be Holloway's and a few other Marines' (Jenkins, Jasso, and Johnson) ticket to sightseeing all over the island. The Marines used their gas rations, Robbie provided the driving, and they could be seen motoring hither and yon over the New Zealand countryside, packed into the little car, and taking in the sights.

Elsie's sister, Bessie, worked in a dress shop and lived in Otaki with her 13-year-old son, Paddy Noble. Paddy's mother had given him a .22 rifle with the stipulation that he could only use it under adult supervision. That's where Stan came in. He would come up for the weekend and take Paddy out to hunt rabbits. Because there were no beasts of prey, the rabbits were everywhere; it was like an infestation. All you had to do was hit them as they were wildly running around. Holloway made sure Paddy handled the rifle safely and that he was close by when firing. After being at Tulagi and Guadalcanal, he did not want to be shot in New Zealand with a .22. Paddy and Stan would skin the rabbits, throw them in a gunnysack, and on the way home they'd give them to people. At that time meat was scarce in New Zealand, all of it going to the boys fighting in the war. The country of New Zealand had put its heart and soul into the war effort. Per capita, they had more fighting men overseas than any other nation.

On one of Stan and Paddy's hunting sojourns an older Maori gentleman, a friend of Robbie's, went with them. He was a husky man with dark, wavy hair, and sported the traditional facial tattoos. As they traipsed along he would sing, and his favorite song was "Now Is The Hour." When it came time to dress out the rabbits he instructed Stan and Paddy on how to skin the animal with a deft snap of the wrist. With some practice, they were able to do it themselves.

Not only was there an abundance of rabbits, but there were quite a lot of pigs there too. They weren't wild boars, but domestic pigs that had somehow become free and thrived in the bush. Those pigs were very crafty. Holloway had been on a couple of hunting parties to get some pigs, but they had come back with nothing. Invariably, looking from one hill to another, you would see a group of pigs rooting around. But when you sneaked over to that spot, they would be gone. Looking back to the hill you came from, there would be a bunch of those wily swine standing around. With binoculars, it seemed as if you could see a smile on their faces. When Holloway remarked on that, the old Maori said, "We'll come back tomorrow and I'll show you how to catch a pig."

The next day Paddy stayed home and Robbie went with Holloway. The Maori brought with him a dog that looked like a bull terrier mix mutt. It was brown with white spots. They walked quite a distance out and up to the crest of a hill and, sure enough, they could see a group of pigs about 200 yards away. Holloway and Robbie turned to the Maori, "Now what do we do?" The old man didn't answer them—he spoke to the dog. Whatever he said, the dog understood and he slipped away silently. "Now, let's go get that pig." After they had walked a short distance, they heard a commotion up ahead. It sounded like the dog had found the pigs. When they reached the spot where they had seen the pigs, all of them were gone—except one. He hadn't been able to go anywhere because he had a dog holding him by the ear. They killed the pig, took it back, and quartered it. Elsie roasted a quarter for Stan to take back to camp. Holloway caught the midnight train back. When he arrived at camp he found an all night poker game going on. He rustled out a cook to get bread and other sandwich makings, and they laid out a tasty spread. Word moved through camp with epidemic speed, and when the poker game broke up in the morning the entire quarter of pork was just a delicious memory.

Everywhere they went the Marines would have one or more poker games going. If in a secure location like aboard ship or in New Zealand, as long as they weren't fighting for their lives, the poker would be hot and heavy. Holloway liked the game and did pretty well at it; he was a cautious player, not winning a lot, but not losing a lot either. Sometimes the men would be out of money, but that didn't stop them. They would play "jawbone" poker. Everyone had a little booklet to keep track of their winnings and, after a winning hand, it would be noted in the little book who owed how much. Each poker-playing marine would carry that booklet with him wherever he went, always ready for a game. However, when it came time to make a push to attack another island, the marines had a tradition that they would all follow. The young men would stand at the railing of the ship, just prior to climbing down the nets or boarding the landing craft, and each would take out his little poker booklet and toss it over the railing into the sea—everybody was even, all debts were wiped out.

Rabbit hunting was fun, and extremely easy. But after a while Holloway decided it might be entertaining to try something different— maybe fishing. He and Paddy started out early to walk the three miles to the Otaki River where they would try their luck. They were ill prepared, bringing only some line, hooks, and flies. The plan was to take their time and cut some willow branches for poles. It was mid-morning when the fishermen reached the river, and they walked along the shore looking for a good fishing spot. The day was overcast with a slight wind. Looking over the water, they could see that it was shallow for most of its 30-foot width and the current produced little riffles on the surface. Holloway drew the last drag on his cigarette and casually flipped it out over the water. The butt landed on the surface and floated for about two seconds—Slosh! A good-sized fish hit it. That action was like a magnet on two sets of eyes, drawing them to the spot.

"Wow, did you see that?!"

"We've got to rig up some poles! Where's a willow tree?"

It was an emergency—and they were scrambling with excitement. If there had been more than just the two of them, they would have looked like the Keystone Cops. The fish gods had been waiting for them to get there, to start reaping the harvest. One simply couldn't make the almighty powers wait any longer!

Holloway tied some line to a pole and put a fly on it. He gave that to Paddy and said "Go get 'em!" Then he quickly outfitted his own. The two happy fishermen started landing 10- to 12-inch trout right away. They never did go hunting again.

It was on a liberty trip to Otaki that Holloway decided to go AWOL (Absent Without Leave). He wasn't deserting, but just staying out an extra day. Word was that the Colonel would be gone and most of the men would be out on a long hike. Maybe they wouldn't even notice. But his absence was noticed, and on his return the next day he was commanded to appear before the Colonel. Sitting behind his desk, the Colonel laid down some papers he had been scrutinizing and looked at the Marine in front of him, standing at attention.

"This is something new for you, Holloway. Did you think you could get by with it?"

"Yes, sir."

"Well, you didn't do it. You didn't get by with it."

Holloway received two week's restriction for that little stunt. More importantly, if he had been close to being promoted to Sergeant, that killed his chances. But Holloway didn't care about promotions anyway; he didn't care to have any authority. Ever since they put a bucket over his head he had been cruising along, getting by, and marking time.

As the outdoors beckoned Holloway on the weekends, so the city attracted Jerry Howery. The major part of the appeal was he was in love. But Holloway claimed "Jerry you're always in love. Every time you see a woman, you're in love."

"No, Stan, this one's different. Marg is really beautiful—she's something special!"

Margaret Stewart

Jerry Howery (left)
and Stan Holloway

"Wellington, New Zealand-
Marines generally stop off at
the American Red Cross
('Cecil Club'), big recreation
center here, before making
the 'last train' back to camp
at the end of a liberty day.
8-29-43"

S/Sgt. R.E. Olund

Howery suggested that on the next liberty Stan take a train ride south with him to Wellington. They would go to the "ANA Club", where Marg was a member.

The ANA was the same club where Stan and Jerry had partied on their first liberty in N.Z. Everything was the same, except maybe there were more people than before. Howery spotted his girlfriend and the two Marines walked across the floor to her. She was beautiful. She was tall and thin with soft brown hair that she had barretted back on one side. Her bright blue eyes seemed to dance with mischief as she and Jerry bantered back and forth. When Jerry introduced them, Stan smiled and said, "Howery has told me about you and, I have to say, I approve of his choice."

The night seemed to fly by and at midnight the young Marines had to leave to catch the train. As the train clip-clapped its way back to camp, Holloway closed his eyes and thought about the perfect time he had had that night. Dancing, chatting, sipping tea and consuming little sandwiches. It would never be forgotten. And Jerry had been right—his girlfriend was really something special.

It wasn't very long after that Jerry got real sick. After he checked into the infirmary, they diagnosed him with malaria and dengue fever and gave him his traveling papers back to the States. All the Marines had become acquainted with the jungle diseases. Both malaria and dengue fever are tropical diseases spread by the mosquito. The symptoms can be similar—high fever, sweats, body aches, severe headache, malaise. With dengue fever, which is often accompanied by a rash, the joints and bones can become very painful, the eyes hurt,

Margaret (r) and Mary Stewart

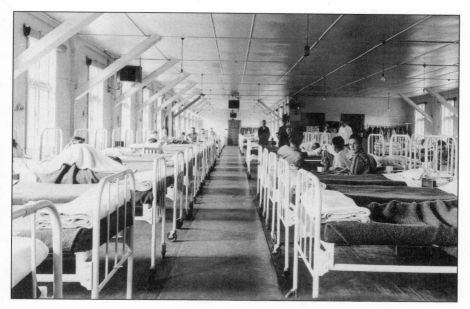

"Silverstream, Wellington. Ward seven (7). July 1943"
S/Sgt. J.H. Sutton, 2nd Marine Div.

and headaches can be excruciating. When Holloway's temperature went up and he started to feel sick he knew what it was. He had initially been hit with malaria while on Tulagi. But malaria doesn't just go away. It sticks around and attacks you again from time to time, which kept Holloway taking atabrin every day. Malaria is not to be taken lightly— he was checked into the hospital at Silverstream. Navy nurses ran the operation there, mostly 1st and 2nd Lieutenants. All of them out-ranked Holloway, a lowly corporal.

Sometimes on weekends the nurses would go out and party on board ship, then come back to the hospital stumbling drunk, ready to raise hell. It was the first weekend Holloway was there when he was awakened in the middle of the night.

"Piss call! Roll out!" Two drunken nurses had turned on the lights and were tromping around waking everyone. One of the nurses came to Holloway's bed and walked up beside him. Holloway was lying on his side with an arm outside the covers. The nurse bent down, took hold of the covers as if to cover his arm, then whipped the sheets and blanket over his head. As surprising as this was, the first thing Holloway noticed was a cool open air feeling on his backside. When the covers were jerked over his head his butt was uncovered and hanging out of his hospital gown. Holloway reached up and pulled the covers down, the nurse yanked them back, and Holloway pulled them down. By this time both of them were throwing some verbiage at each other. Holloway grasped the covers while telling the nurse to get away from him. As she struggled to pull the bedding from him, she reminded him of his rank and her rank. His behavior was clear-cut insubordination. Finally, she gave up and left the floor.

Holloway wouldn't get back to sleep right away. He lay there wondering if she would write him up. Maybe this was a new type of therapy to help malaria patients recover faster. It didn't seem to be working. The middle-of-the-night exertion had spiked his temperature and he felt queasy. The next morning the doctor made his rounds, examining patients and talking with them. With him was the head nurse. Holloway watched them work their way around the ward. His bed was one of the last ones they would visit. The doctor looked at his chart. "How are you feeling, Holloway?"

"I'm ready to go back to camp."

The doctor looked surprised. "Oh, no. You're not going back to camp."

"If I stay here one more night I'm apt to kill a nurse." He told the doctor about the previous night's "tug-of-war" game with his bedding. The doctor's expression didn't divulge what he would do about the incident, if anything. He finished the examination then visited the last two beds to complete his rounds. Holloway watched the doctor walk down the hallway away from the ward. He turned the corner to his office and disappeared. A few minutes later an orderly appeared by Holloway's bed. "Get your things together, Holloway. We're moving you." Holloway was sent to the hospital at Camp Anderson, which was run by male Navy corpsmen. It was a nice facility. Holloway looked out the window from his hospital bed and could see the lovely botanical gardens below. He knew he would like it there. The corpsmen were nice.

They had a policy whereby patients who were able could earn privileges by helping out. Holloway would clean windows or maybe mop floors. In turn he was able to go on liberty any evening he felt able. Despite the amenities, Holloway began to feel lonely. His buddy, Howery, who could always liven things up, was now back in the States. But what really needled at him was that he couldn't stop thinking about Jerry's girlfriend, Marg. Yes, she was lovely. But, what Holloway found most appealing was the way he felt so comfortable when with her. Even though he had only conversed with her several times throughout that evening, he felt as if he could spend hours with her, just talking about... everything. He remembered that night that he'd met her, Howery was talking about a time that he had called Marg on the phone. Telling the story, Howery had mentioned her phone number—16510. Holloway was very good at remembering numbers, and this one he locked away in his cranium, never to be forgotten.

He was somewhat nervous about calling the number. All he knew was her first name. If she wasn't there and he had to leave a message, he wasn't sure what it would be. She may not even remember him. He dialed the number—16510. It rang several times—maybe this wasn't such a good...

"Hello" It was a woman, maybe her mother.

"Hi. Is Marg there?" Please say yes! Please say yes!

"Just a moment. I'll get her."

After a brief interlude, "Hello, this is Marg."

Indeed, she did remember him. Stan told her about the malaria and about the hospital. He was elated when she offered to come out and see him. In fact, she came for a visit the next day and they had a nice time talking, getting acquainted. As Marg got up to leave, Stan asked her if she could visit again soon.

"I could come out on Saturday."

"That would be great."

"Can I bring you anything, Stan?"

After a moment's pause, "Yes, a pumpkin pie would sure be nice."

That next Saturday Marg arrived with a fresh baked pumpkin pie. Having never made one before, she used Auntie Chris's recipe, tried to follow it exactly, and the pie looked good. Marg divided it up so that each of the six men on that end of the ward got a slice. Holloway loved pumpkin pie. His mother used to make the best. He took a bite and closed his eyes as he chewed to relish the flavor of that lovely pie. Wait a minute! Something was wrong—this pie tasted dreadful! Stan looked at Marg sitting by the bed, smiling at him. He smiled back.

"Say, Marg, this is really good!" one of the other guys exclaimed.

"Really delicious pie, Marg."

Maybe she had forgotten to include sugar or maybe she had used a squash by mistake, but it didn't matter. All of the men were chiming in, complimenting Marg on how tasty the pie was.

When Marg left that afternoon, Stan watched her leave the building and walk down the street. Except for the soft whirring of a fan and the sound of an orderly mopping at the other end of the ward, the area was quiet. When everyone was sure that Marg was gone and out of earshot, the barrage hit. They threw shoes and anything else they could get hold of.

"Holloway, if I could get out of bed I'd strangle you!"

"That was the worst pie I've ever had!"

"Don't ever ask her to cook anything again!"

While still at the hospital, Holloway had recuperated enough that he was allowed out on liberty. Even if he didn't have liberty, the orderlies showed him how to take liberty anyway by exiting the rear of the hospital and detouring around the front gate by way of climbing over an outcropping of rocks. So he could leave whenever he wished. He walked to downtown Wellington, then caught a taxi to Marg's house at 155 Seatoun Heights. After Holloway was discharged from the hospital, he was able to make it to Wellington several times to see Marg. Each time the same hack driver would be there to give him a ride. On one occasion Stan met Mrs. Stewart (Marg's mother) in downtown Wellington and they shared the cab ride. As they were getting out of the cab, Stan pulled out a one pound note for the driver—which was the normal charge. Mrs. Stewart asked what he was doing, as the normal fare should be about one third of a pound. He explained that he'd always paid a pound to this hack driver. Holloway could see an instant change in Mrs. Stewart's countenance. Her smiling friendly face disappeared, replaced by a very serious look. He had seen the same expression before on his mother's face. It meant someone was going to get a whipping. Mrs. Stewart turned to the driver.

"You dirty thief! How dare you rob these boys!" That was just the beginning. A tongue-lashing can be a verbal thing of beauty when done by a master. Mrs. Stewart gave no quarter as she chastised the dishonest reprobate. Holloway had to smile to himself as he watched the driver, holding the steering wheel with both hands and seeming to sink into his seat.

It was in New Zealand that Holloway first came in contact with the Red Cross. They had just finished up with Guadalcanal and were arriving in N.Z. when the Red Cross rewarded their efforts by handing out cartons of cigarettes. They documented the names of the Marines and how many cartons each received. At that time the Marines could buy cigarettes at the ship's store for 5 cents a pack, or 50 cents a carton. So they were surprised when they received their next paycheck to find their pay had been docked for the cigarettes—at $2.50 per carton. The Red Cross continued to play that little game throughout the war. They would always find some new service men who didn't know about them.

The pay line always went in alphabetical order. If your name started with A you would get paid first. Standing in line with the H's, Holloway heard some of the men, who had received their pay, grumbling about something. They were saying, "We just donated to the Red Cross." When it was Holloway's turn, the paymaster said, "You are making a contribution to the Red Cross, right?"

"What if I don't want to?" Holloway asked.

"You don't have to, but we'll sure make you wish you had" was the reply he got. Holloway had heard this phrase several times in the Marines. So he volunteered to give a portion of his paycheck to the Red Cross. It made him wonder how many people were involved in the scheme. Some officers must be cooperating, maybe getting a slice of the pie. In fact, as entrenched as the Red Cross seemed to be with the upper brass, some people must have been getting rich. The victims of these programs were military personnel that the Red Cross was supposed to be helping.

Later, in Hawaii, Stan would have another experience with the Red Cross. As the result of some poor planning and brash foolishness, Holloway once found himself in Hilo, Hawaii, without any money and no place to stay. But he did notice a Red Cross office and decided to see if they could help him out. He explained his predicament to the woman behind the desk and was told yes, they could assist him. But first he must fill out some paperwork authorizing a small loan, which would be payable with interest, plus a loan fee. They could provide him with a bed at a price, and the same terms of payment would apply. Holloway politely declined and left.

About a block down the street was a Salvation Army office. Why not give it a try? The building was a large warehouse-looking place, and when Stan entered he could see they had numerous bunks there. The lady at the desk near the door listened to his story and told him yes, they could help him out. He could sleep there. She reached into a drawer and pulled out a $5 bill. Handing it to him, she said, "This will help you get some food, since we don't have a cafeteria." Stan asked if she would need his name, or if he would have to sign anything. And was told "No, we are a beneficent organization. We are here to help you."

After resting there for about nine months, the Marines' stay in N.Z. was coming to a close. The war was demanding fuel, both human and machinery. "We're going aboard ship" was what they were told. They were also instructed to turn in all their uniforms to be stored on the ship, leaving them with only their dungarees. The dungarees were their every day clothes, especially in combat.

Holloway wanted to make one more trip into Wellington to see Marg. But he would have to figure out a way. First, he borrowed clothes from a guy named Margolin who was staying behind in the rear echelon. Margolin was bigger than Holloway, but the clothes would be passable. The rest of the plan was to walk in to Plimmerton and catch a train to Wellington. Strolling down the road, Holloway listened for approaching vehicles and several times had to jump off the road and hide as jeeps drove by. They carried colonels or captains who would kick his butt right back to camp. In one open space of road Holloway heard a jeep approaching from camp. There was nowhere to hide—he just stood there. The jeep came to a stop in a cloud of dust and Stan heard, "Where are you going, Holloway? Standing on the shoulder of the road, Holloway looked at the lone person in the jeep and recognized him as Captain Jones. He had been caught and there was no use lying about it.

"I'm going into Wellington, sir."

"Well, hop in. That's where I'm goin' too."

Holloway couldn't believe his good fortune. He jumped into the seat. As the jeep lurched forward, Captain Jones asked, "Why are you going in to Wellington?"

Stan looked at him and said, "I'm in love."

The captain smiled as he gazed down the road. "So am I."

The narrow paved road had light traffic that morning. Green pastures sprawled on both sides, with grazing sheep and an occasional cluster of farm buildings. They passed through some small seaside towns and, as the jeep slowly ate up the miles, the two Marines had a real good visit. Normally, talking to an officer meant limiting your side of the conversation to "yes, sir" and "no, sir." But today they were two Marines talking about girls, home, where they'd go next. Holloway felt that if they had met under different conditions they might have been good friends.

Jones was good to his word. In fact, he drove Holloway right to Marg's doorstep. They saluted each other and the captain drove away.

Marg and Stan spent a quiet day together. They walked down Seatoun Heights to their favorite spot—a little bench overlooking Worser Bay. Snuggled together, they talked—about their families, about the present. But both Marg and Stan knew better than to discuss any future plans. The whole world was in turmoil. It was going to be a long war and to talk of the future would only invite hopes and dreams to be shattered.

That night Stan stayed at the Stewart's. In the morning Mrs. Stewart fixed breakfast for them, then the young couple walked to the bottom of the hill to catch the tram car. Marg was having to go to work. It was a lovely, bright morning. Stan stood holding the pole in the tram car as Marg sat in one of the seats facing across the front of the car. Stan leaned close to her. "Would you go to Otaki with me?" It would be a nice getaway for a day. But Marg was supposed to go to work. She had never missed work like that.

"No, Stan, I have to go to work."

But Stan was persistent. It was a beautiful day for an outing; why not make the best of it? Try as he may, he couldn't talk her into it. The woman sitting next to Marg, someone she didn't know, said, "Oh, for goodness sake, *go!*"

They called Mrs. Stewart from the train station and asked her to call Marg's work for her. Then they rode the train to Otaki, where they spent a delightful day visiting with Robbie and Elsie, and seeing the sights in the little town.

That was the last time they would see each other for three years. When Marg kissed Stan goodbye that evening and stepped into her house, she remarked to her mother, "Look, Mum, Stan left his necktie." It was hanging in the hallway where he'd left it. But Stan was gone. That necktie would remain hanging in the hallway for years. New Zealand had been good to Holloway and the other Marines. In fact, some of them decided they would stay there. They were casualties to love. Everything they had wanted was there; it was like heaven. There were the forests and plenty of good hunting, lots of fishing for everything from trout to swordfish, plenty of city life in the good-sized city of Wellington. Add falling head over heels in love with a beautiful N.Z. girl and that could make the allure of the country too much to resist. As far as Holloway was concerned, the only drawback was the cold winter weather. There was a wind that they called the "southerly buster" that would combine with the rain to chill a person to the bone. Holloway had spent some four-hour shifts on guard duty walking around the camp, wearing everything he owned, and completely wet. That was the coldest he would ever be in his life. But the winter weather was not a big deficit. You would just spend that time indoors, as the Marines had done, maybe listening to Tom Enos work his magic with the clarinet and dancing at the Hotel Cecil.

Unfortunately for the Marines that decided not to get on the ship, the Marine Corps did not view their staying in N.Z. from a romantic standpoint. That was desertion. One person that Holloway knew had gone over the hill was their Laundry NCO. He was a very nice guy who had fallen in love and made a poor choice to desert. Later Holloway would hear it announced that that love-struck Marine had been sentenced to 50 years at Mare Island Prison.

The next day the Marines went aboard ship, where they would stay until they shipped out. They weren't allowed to go into town. That's why Holloway was so surprised when his friend, "Ike" Iconelli said, "Stan, let's go into town."

"What are you talking about, Ike? We can't get off the ship."

"Don't worry. I'll take care of that."

Holloway looked at the city-smart Italian. He didn't know what he had up his sleeve, but if it called for toughness and guts, Iconelli was the guy to do it.

"Even if we did get off the ship, I'm broke. On top of that, I'm not feeling all that great."

Sitting on his bunk near them was Norbert Fiedler. He'd been keeping busy cutting hair and had saved up some money. "If Ike can pull it off, I'll give you the money, Stan." There wasn't much left to ponder. Holloway knew that this would be his last chance to see Marg. "Okay, let's go!"

Before they were in sight of the gate Ike said, "Stan, just march straight for the gate." Then he started loudly calling cadence, "HUT, TWO, HUT, TWO, HUT, TWO..."

Holloway was marching with Ike matching step right behind him. He could see the guard, standing with a rifle across his chest, blocking the exit. They were marching right at him. "HUT, TWO, HUT, TWO..." When the two marching Marines were within ten feet of the guard, Ike barked at him, "ONE MAN WORKING PARTY!"

Holloway was like a human freight train, intending to keep marching if he had to walk right over the top of that guard. The guard had less than two seconds to make a decision—either block their exit or get the hell out of the way. He stepped aside. Stan and Ike kept marching right up Willis Street to the ANA Club. They'd made it. It was time to have some fun. Stan immediately called Marg at work and asked her to come to the club. But Marg had made other plans. "I'm sorry, Stan, I've arranged to meet some people for lunch. I just can't come down today." Holloway told her how much he wanted to see her, to be with her. But, at the last moment he decided not to play his trump card—he wouldn't tell her that this would be their last chance to get together before the ship left with him on it. She knew he would be leaving, but not how soon. No, he didn't tell her. He didn't have her break her plans so that he could gaze into those lovely eyes and dance a few last dances. He didn't because, by now, he was starting to feel very sick. His head was thumping and his eyes were aching. He would have to get into the infirmary soon. So he said his fond farewells and walked back to the ship and the infirmary.

———

Chapter
FOUR

—

The next day the ship left Wellington. The Marines had no idea where they were going and Holloway didn't care. He was diagnosed with dengue fever. His eyes and head throbbed painfully, and all of his bones and joints ached. The corpsmen pampered him and treated him as if he were going to die, and Holloway felt as if he were going to die.

> *155 Seatoun Hgts Rd.*
> *Wellington. E.5.*
> *31st October, 1943*
>
> *Dearest Stan,*
>
> *Well, I guess Wednesday night was the last night we will see each other for a long time. It was a pity things were so abrupt at the end and I'm glad you got back by 11.0 as we were a bit worried about it. I wish now that I'd gone to lunch with you on Friday but I thought I'd be seeing you yesterday. As things turned out I didn't and it was a funny thing but both Mum and I had an idea that you wouldn't be coming. I've been thinking of you a lot yesterday and*

today and I'm wondering where you are. If you are having weather like we are having you shouldn't be at all seasick. It's so lovely and hot I'm writing this down in the back yard and I'm trying to get my legs brown but it's going to be a bit of a job. Still, when I go on my holiday I should get lovely and brown. Optimistic, aren't I? I'm going to miss you more than I can say, Stan. And yesterday I moped around like a cat that's lost its kittens. This afternoon Mum, Mary and I are going to the Botanical Gardens and it should be very beautiful up there.

Stan, I'm writing a (?) letter. I know, and I wish I could write as well as you do. You write such lovely love letters (how's that for alliteration?) and you must have a lot of thoughts in that head of yours. Napoleon was pretty good at love letters, I believe. Not that I put you in the same class as him although he was brainy but I think you have as many brains of any man I know. I had my hair done on Friday night but it wasn't much good because my hair is too soft and directly I got outside it all fell out. You'll have to excuse the writing but this is being balanced very precariously on my knees and the sun is so strong that one of my eyes is all screwed up.

I'll sign off now and write to you again soon and I'll be waiting to hear from you.

With lots of love, Stan, and please keep yourself safe and well.

Margaret

The ship's first stop was New Hebrides to pick up more fleet, and it seemed as if everything that could float was there. There were carriers, battleships, and cruisers as far as you could see. From New Hebrides they sailed directly to Tarawa Atoll, in the Gilbert Islands. Tarawa consists of 47 small coral islands of which Betio (pronounced BAY-shee-o) is the largest. Almost all the fighting would take place on Betio, which is about 2 1/2 miles long and 800 yards wide at its widest part, or about the size of New York's Central Park. The code name for the operation was "Helen", but the battle would be known as "Tarawa." The Japanese had fortified Betio with bombproof blockhouses, pillboxes, and bunkers, making that the heart of their defense. They had almost 5,000 men, most of them their toughest and well-trained Imperial Marines. The Japanese commander there had boasted, "A million men cannot take Tarawa in a hundred years." The Second Division Marines were going to prove him wrong.

By the time they arrived at Tarawa, Holloway had pretty well shaken the ill effects of dengue fever. The sickness would not kill him after all. The aches and pains had subsided and the blinding headaches had gone away.

Before the Marines could see Tarawa, they could hear the bombardment of it. U.S. ships were blasting away and dive-bombers were dropping bombs on the island. As they got closer they were able to see the dark shape on the horizon. It was on fire, with flames jumping into the sky and billowing smoke, forming a hazy shroud around the island. This was going to be their new accommodations for the near future, if they were lucky. If not, it would serve as their funeral pyre. As they got closer they could see, hear, and feel the concussion of the bombs. (As it turned out, the bombing and shelling didn't produce the results they had wanted. The bombproof bunkers and pillboxes were constructed in an oval concrete shell design, so anything but a direct hit would ricochet off. Sixteen-inch shells would glance off and land in the ocean. The enemy would be there in full force when the Marines landed.) At the same time, the Japanese were firing back with their big guns, but that effort seemed ineffectual compared to the guns of the fleet.

Early in the morning of November 20, 1943, Holloway stood at the ship's rail with the other Marines and watched the bombing of the island. Just off the beaches they could see small structures positioned the full length of where they would eventually land and were told not to worry, "Those are latrines."

The first bunch of Marines hustled down the cargo nets, dropped into landing craft, and began to churn back and forth in the water, waiting for the order to proceed to the beach. With them in the water were amphibious tanks, or LVTs (tracked landing vehicle), called "alligators." As Holloway looked out toward the island, he could see what looked like a jumbled mass of Higgins boats and LVTs, motoring around in every direction. He knew that he would joining them shortly. By that time, the men were anxious. They were tired of waiting. Hopefully, after all that shelling and bombing, there wouldn't be anyone there to put up any resistance.

The first wave received the order to move and they began motoring toward the island. They made it to within several hundred yards of the beach when something went wrong. The Higgins boats could go no further. They were designed to propel through the water and dump the troops out at the beach. But the water was too shallow—they were hung up and would have to dump the troops where they were. That meant the Marines would have to wade over a quarter of a mile in waist to chest deep water. The brass had neglected to note that there was a low tide, or, if they knew about it, they decided the water would not be low enough to ground the landing craft on the reef. But that wasn't the only surprise. As the marines tediously walked through the deep water they encountered another revelation that made the landing much more deadly. The "latrines" lined up on the beach were actually machine gun positions. The first wave of Marines made it about half way to the beach before the Japanese machine guns began firing on them.

For purposes of planning, the beach marked for the landing was divided into three objective assault areas—from right to left, Red Beach

One, Red Beach Two, and Red Beach Three. Separating Two and Three was a pier about 700 yards long. In the first wave was Col. David M. Shoup, Commander of the 2nd Marine Division. He jumped out of his LVT and was immediately shot in the leg. He painfully waded toward the relative safety of the pier, then looked around at what was left of his men, clinging to the pier. They had been shocked and demoralized at the ferocity of the fire they had just jumped into. The first thing Shoup did was try to establish radio contact with the other landing teams under his command. Major John F. Schoettel, was landing on Red Beach One. The following is their communication:

Schoettel: "Receiving heavy fire all along beach. Unable to land all. Issue in doubt."

Schoettel: (eight minutes later) "Boats held up on reef of right flank Red One. Troops receiving heavy fire in water."

Shoup: (eight minutes later) "Land Beach Red Two and work west."

Schoettel: (three minutes later) "We have nothing left to land."[1]

The Marines who made it to the beach sea wall were trapped. They were pinned down and needed help. If there had been any way to pull all the survivors off the island and rethink the whole plan, the officers in command probably would have done it. But that was not possible. And just leaving them there was not an option. The only thing left was to pour more Marines into the deadly path of those Japanese machine guns positioned up and down the full length of the beach. And that's what they did.

Holloway was one of those Marines in a following wave. He scrambled down the net into the Higgins boat and looked around at the other men. Sergeant Grivitch was there. Most of the others were newer replacements for those killed or wounded at Guadalcanal or Tulagi or sent home for some other reason. He could see they were all scared. Some were praying, others were huddled, trying to keep their fear to themselves. There were a couple of "See ya on the beach, Mac." But, for the most part, they were silent.

[1] Rafael Steinberg and the Editors of Time-Life Books, *Island Fighting*, 1978, p. 112.

At Tulagi the Marines didn't know that much about the enemy and when they landed it was with some bravado. They had been ready to kick some butt. But this was different. They knew they were going into a hellish situation and they knew the Japanese would fight to the death. Holloway was scared too.

It was almost dusk when the landing craft stopped and dumped them out into the water—it was over waist deep. Everyone was hollering or screaming over the background noise of the Japanese machine guns spitting hot death at them. Holloway was yelling too. He couldn't help it. His body was producing so much adrenaline that his vocal chords had to get into the act. The result was a mix of possibly a primal war cry and a scream of total terror. Machine gun bullets were skipping off the water all around him, some only inches away. He would hear a distinctive WHUMP and know that one of the other men had been hit. Sometimes they would cry out before they died. But usually they'd just silently slide beneath the surface of the water. To make things worse, the hulk of the *Nimonea*, a freighter that had been knocked over by a U.S. destroyer before the invasion, sat about 200 yards out and was full of Japanese machine gunners and riflemen, firing at the Marines from behind.

In the air, reconnaissance planes watched the tragedy unfold. Lt. Cdr. Robert A. MacPherson was flying a Vought-Sikorsky Type OS2U Kingfisher observation aircraft. Earlier in the day, when the assault began, Rear Admiral Harry W. Hill had anxiously asked him if the landing craft were able to make it over the reef. His sad reply was "Negative." He would report later: "The water never seemed clear of tiny men, their rifles held over their heads, slowly wading beachward. I wanted to cry."[2]

Hundreds of yards in front of Holloway was Red Beach Two. As he looked at the beach he noticed a little bit to the left was a pier jutting out quite a distance. If he could make it to that pier maybe he could somehow get to the beach. That would certainly be better than where he was now—out in the open water. It was slow going walking through

---

[2] Col. Joseph H. Alexander, USMC (Ret.), *Utmost Savagery, The Three Days of Tarawa*, Ivy Books, pp. 6-7.

the almost chest deep water. He wanted to move quickly, but that was impossible. Every second under machine gun fire seemed like an eternity. When he reached the pier he hugged up against it in hopes that it would offer some protection. Staying as close as he could to the pier, he worked his way up to the beach and finally to the sea wall. Sitting in the dark, with his back against the sea wall Holloway found prayer. He had never been much of a praying person. He hadn't prayed at Tulagi or Guadalcanal. In fact, Holloway hadn't recited prayers since he was a little boy saying "Now I lay me down to sleep..." But here at Tarawa he prayed, "Please, God, I want to live."

Rear Admiral Shibasaki had planned the Japanese defenses very well. Their plan was to mow down the Marines, keep them at the seawall, then wipe them out that night with a counterattack.

But the counterattack didn't materialize. Holloway and the other exhausted Marines, scattered in a disorganized line against the seawall, were spared certain death. Historians have debated the reason why there was no counter attack. A contributing factor had to have been that the Japanese landline communication system had been destroyed by the heavy naval and aerial bombardment. The Japanese command couldn't get word to their troops to attack. But now historians believe that the main reason for the Japanese inaction that first night was that Commander Shibasaki and his staff died on the first day of the assault. Initially, he was thought to have died on the third day. However, evidence and personal accounts confirm that Shibasaki was moving with his staff from one bunker to another and was caught in the open by a large shell, killing them all. Shibasaki had been the inspirational leader of the Japanese forces on Betio and, with his death, they were stunned. There was no one to order the counterattack.[3]

Some of the Japanese gun placements were moved that night and some of the Japanese soldiers sneaked through the Marines to reestablish well-armed machine gun nests in the remains of some disabled LVTs, and in the rusting hulk of the Nimonea. When dawn

[3] Col. Joseph H. Alexander, USMC (Ret.), *Utmost Savagery, The Three Days of Tarawa*, Ivy Books, pp. 157-161.

broke, Holloway and the other Marines seemed to be under fire from four different directions. As the navy scrambled to knock out those machine guns in the water, and planes dropped bombs on them, Holloway climbed over the seawall.

Holloway would make it over the seawall but much of his memory of Tarawa would be a haze of death and burning hell. The Marines fought their way literally foot by foot, taking out the big blockhouses, small pillboxes, and staggered rows of machine gun nests one by one with flame throwers, hand grenades, explosives, and rifle fire. Some tanks, equipped with flame throwers, were brought in to help blast away and burn out the fortifications. As the situation worsened for the Japanese, they began killing themselves with hand grenades or their own rifles. They tried several counterattacks, but their efforts were useless against the advancing Marines. Many were blown up or burned to death in their bunkers. Of the 4,836 Japanese on the island, only 17 soldiers were taken prisoner.

Tarawa would go down as the bloodiest battle in Marine Corps history. The Marine dead were so numerous that in order to maneuver a boat between the little island of Bairiki and Betio the bodies had to be poled out of the way. Holloway spent some time between the two islands moving ammunition and transporting prisoners. On one excursion he accompanied a prisoner in a small Navy boat. They didn't have far to go but it took awhile with all the bodies in the way. The Navy boys wanted to kill the prisoner.

"Just turn your head for a minute and we'll take care of him." But Holloway wouldn't do it. He told them, "No. I'm delivering him in one piece and alive." He didn't blame them. In fact, Holloway was very tempted to kill the prisoner himself. There was that much hate in him. He would never have believed that he could feel that way. Holloway had been given orders to accompany and deliver the prisoner and Marines always follow orders. It didn't matter how he felt or others felt, he would not disobey an order.

The Marines had set up artillery on Bairiki Island and ammo was brought from there to Betio. The water was so shallow that you could almost walk between the islands. Holloway helped with lugging the ammo, while wading in waist-deep water filled with dead Marines. The stench was horrific. It was an effort to breathe. The smell of the decomposing bodies would catch in the throat and, after throwing up everything in the stomach, the gag reflex kept trying to summon up more. The sun blazed down on them with a ferocity that Holloway had never experienced before. He had his shirt off and the sun rays blistered his back and shoulders right through his already deep tan.

———

Up until that point the newspaper and film reports of the war had been somewhat watered down. With the attack on the Gilbert Islands (Tarawa) the Marines decided to give the press full rein to accompany troops and report on the combat as they wished. This changed the whole outlook of the war for the public back home in the States. When the news reports started coming back to the U.S., people were shocked. They had never before heard of the Gilbert Islands, much less Tarawa, and now they were hearing that so many of their boys had died there. The Marine Corps came under intense pressure from the Navy, the Roosevelt administration, and the press to release the casualty figures. After delaying for about a week, the Marine Corps publicized the figures. In 76 hours of fighting there were over 3,000 casualties with over 1,000 dead.

In addition, a documentary had been filmed during the battle entitled *With the Marines at Tarawa* showing the reality and ugliness of the fighting. President Roosevelt agonized over whether or not to release the film. He knew that if the documentary were shown in movie theaters it could dramatically spark sales of war bonds, which were lagging. But Roosevelt also feared that it might be too graphic for the general public. Needing some expert advice, he privately conferred with Robert Sherrod, a *Time-Life* journalist who had just come back from the battlefield. Sherrod felt that the American people knew very little about the realities of fighting against the Japanese and he recommended releasing it in its entirety. Roosevelt took his advice and released the documentary. *With the Marines at Tarawa* became an overnight sensation and won an Academy Award. For the first time, the American people saw a true picture of what their boys were going through on those Pacific islands. One particular scene toward the end had a horrifying and sobering effect on people back home. It showed dead Marines lying on the beach and half floating in the surf. As a result, the sale of war bonds spiked upward and the recruitment into the Marine Corps dropped significantly.

———

Lost mementos on Tarawa beach

When the Marines left New Zealand they were sorely missed. Sweethearts and others wrote letters to them in prolific fashion. In the months and years following, the Marines built a reputation of being, at best, sporadic in answering the letters, but they loved to receive them and the people back in the States and in New Zealand kept writing to keep the boys' spirits up. Even though he didn't write back often,

Holloway always enjoyed hearing from home and from the people in New Zealand. Marg and her mother, Dorothy, wrote at least twice a week. He also heard from Marg's younger sister, Mary, her brother, Alan, Elsie (in Otaki) and several others. He even heard from Marg's brother, Doug, who was stationed at Guadalcanal and, later, Bougainville.

29th Nov., 1943

Darling Stan,

Home again and no letters from you. I do wish I might even get just a little line or two so let me know how you are making out. Today's papers reported the dreadful news about the Gilbert Islands and, of course, I've been thinking about you all day. Believe me when I say, my dearest, that I'd give ten years of my life to know how you are. I'd give anything to have you back in New Zealand or to know that you are safe and sound. My imagination does not go far enough for me to realize what a hell you boys are going through and I want you to know, Stan, that our thoughts are with you. I have just had two letters from Jerry and he says that he has not yet received any letters from you. I am telling him that you have written and that you have by no means let him down.

Tonight I must write to Elsie and I would like to go and see her one of these days. Only, of course, I shall not take the day off and get caught doing it like I remember one Marine persuaded me to. Do you recall that? There's a dance down at the Hotel Cecil tonight but I didn't go because I've just caught rather a bad cold and, besides that, my nose is peeling from the sun burn and I look such a sight that I'd be a wall-flower all night.

I shall sign off now, my dearest, and I do hope this finds you well and happy. Christmas is getting pretty near now so I shall wish you a Merry Christmas and a very happy new year.

With lots and lots of love and kisses,

Margaret

P.S. Hope the censors don't take this off you or that it melts.

155 Seatoun Heights Rd
Seatoun
Wellington E.5.
3rd Dec. 1943

Dear Stan,

Just a few lines to let you know that we are all thinking a lot about you, & pray & hope that you are safe & well. We heard some very disturbing news this week about the U.S.A. Marines at Gilbert Island & we are wondering if you were there Stan, & we have all been as miserable as we can be, especially Margaret. She is just longing for a letter from you, so please write to her as often as you can. This war is the very devil, & I am afraid it will be a very sad Xmas for quite a lot of people. Margaret got back from her holiday last Saturday morning & came back with a dreadful cold. I am taking her to the doctors next week, as I think she needs a tonic. Alan was home last week end & is looking very brown & well. The weather here has been lovely this last week or so, but today it is raining, but, still very warm. I don't suppose you would think so, after the heat that you must be having. Mary's school closes tomorrow week for 7 weeks & you may be sure she is very pleased about it & so am I. There is really no news to tell you so will bring this scribble to a close. Everyone says a big Hello. Write soon Stan & may God bless & take care of you. I remain

Yours truly
D.E. Stewart

811 Monroe St.
Stillwater, Okla.

December 30, 1943

Dear Marg,

I'm Stan Holloway's sister. Yesterday I got a letter from him and he kinda wanted me to write to you so here goes. As an added incentive, he mentioned that you might be able to tell me more about him than he could. Could you or would you? Why was he in the hospital last Fall? He hasn't been seriously hurt, has he? He said that you were so good to him while he was sick and he appreciated it more than anyone would ever know. His letter was pretty full of you and he sounded happier than he has in several years. Thank you, Marg, for that.

Well, at the present moment, I am in the hospital with a new son. I'm thrilled and happy as a lark. Our first baby was a girl. She's almost three now and now I have a son and I certainly feel that God has been good to me.

Garsh, what would you like to hear about? I've never tackled a letter like this before. Stan says you excelled in sports but I can't talk to you about that 'cause I'm the world's worst sportswoman except from the grandstand. Bill and I seldom miss a football game and we like basketball, he loves wrestling (he used to do it in college) we like tennis (but he won't play with me. He says he has to have some competition to make the game interesting.) I took two years of it in college but just aren't a good player. He loves to swim, hunt and fish. I go with him but don't do much actual participating.

Stan has probably told you that Bill is a welding professor here at A.&M. Well, our college is so small and the Engineering Dept. practically isn't, for our boys are all in the Service. The college has been turned over to the Army and Navy and Bill is teaching Army Specialized Training Students, Physics, Metalography and Welding. It keeps him pretty busy but he finds it interesting. We have Waves, Radar sailors, Air Corps and the A.S.T.P. students here and our peaceable little college town just is plumb full of Service People.

We have had snow here for several days and now we have a silver thaw in process. It is beautiful. This hospital is out away from other buildings with fields all around. Oklahoma is real flat with nary a mountain and we can see so far. Today the fields look like lakes as the sun melts the snow. I miss the mountains of the West and hate the heat here for a couple of months each summer but the rest of the time is wonderful. I think Stan would like it. Do you know that it's been three years since I've seen him? At one time, we were pretty inseparable and even went on our kid dates together. Sometimes I wonder if we'll ever be together again.

Marg, I'd love to hear from you if you'd care to write.

Sincerely,
Calla Rice

Hq. & Ser. Bat, 3rd Bn, 10th Marines
c/o Fleet P.O. San Francisco, Calif.

December 31, 1943

My Darling Marg,

I was beginning to think you had forgotten me until I got three letters from you today. I hope I have a lot more coming. They're the most anxiously waited for letters I get. I know how tired you get reading love letters but this one must be the "sugar report" kind because that is the way I feel about you. Marg, I had no idea I would ever miss or yearn for anyone like I do you. I've always been pretty serious about you, Darling, but I'm learning the hard way now that "absence makes the heart grow fonder." I wish you cared even half as much as I do for you. Anyway I don't have to remind you that no one else would ever treat you any better than I would. It's terrible to be so crazy about anyone when she's so far away, but God and you willing I'll be back for you. Yes, I still daydream, but am afraid my daydreams are a little over ambitious. If they weren't you'd have the best of everything. I'd sure like to have a chance to try to make them all true. I'm quite ambitious and might surprise you how hard I'd try. I wish I had been with you on your vacation. I'm sure we'd have had fun. I hope you had a lot of fun even though you did sunburn your legs. We never saw all our summer plans develop did we, dearest? Naturally I saw that full moon you mentioned. In fact I leaned on the rail and watched it and thought of you. Wondered what you was doing. You may not believe this but many nights I stood on deck and daydreamed about you until after midnight. We had a different reaction concerning that moon though. Yours you say was romantic. My reaction was just sadness. I couldn't help but feel like the bottom had dropped out of my dream-boat, but I've got it repaired now, and I'm making more plans than ever. Of course you're the hub in my plan wheel. Gerald has written to me several times since I've been here. He still ranks top among my buddies. You asked about his age. He is 23 yrs. old, ten mo. younger than I am.

Your dreams interest me but I'm not superstitious about dreams. I think they are just caused by something being foremost in your mind. That's why I dream about you every night. I'm glad you're reading books on good old U.S.A. If I get my wish you'll be there sometime. I wish you could have seen Mom's last letter. She is as happy as can be about you. Aunt Mildred is a little jealous but very sweet about my losing my head and heart over a girl overseas. I hope she writes to you. She ranks next to you and Mom. You've noticed I call my mother "Mom." You know that's what all the young people at home call her. She's so good to them and they all know and like her as you would if you knew her.

Well my adorable young lady I guess I've bothered you enough for this time. I hope you are all well and happy. Give my best regards to all. You have a family to be proud of, especially your Mum.

In closing, sweetheart, I will just remind you that words can't express my love for you.

Love
Stan

Amity, Ore
Mar. 24, 1944

Dear Margaret:

You'll let me call you that won't you? All my children brought their friends home and I called them by their first names and they called me "mom" until I am "mom" to half the town. I was ever so glad to get your letter. Stan had told me a great deal about you. Poor kid he seems to have drawn a very unlucky number as far as hard battles are concerned. Wally left yesterday. He was happy to go but poor June (his wife) was broken hearted. Calla says Bill has to take his physical the 7th of April. As soon as school is out, I'll go get her and her two babies. Billy Clyde came the day before Christmas and Sharon (Sherry as we all call her) was three years old Jan. 24th. Norman (Sponcy) is still at Vancouver. Today is his birthday. He is twenty years old and has been in the Army a year today. He expects to be sent over some time soon. He said the other day, "Wouldn't it be fun if I was stationed in New Zealand. Then I'd see Stan's sweetie and tease him." Ha! Ha! I am still teaching although spring makes me long to be home and out doors working. My daffodils, violets, and primroses are beautiful and the rose bushes are budding now. Most everyone has their early gardens up but I don't

expect to put mine in for two weeks yet. I am hoping Stanley can get a furlough soon and I want the place shining when he comes home.

Well, dear, I must close for I must write to Stan tonight. Do write again and thanks a million for being so good to Stan while he was there.

Love
Leda M. Holloway

P.S. Give my love to your mother.

Holloway experienced a terror at Tarawa that he would never experience again. He couldn't really explain how he had survived with so many others dying around him. He would storm other beaches and be under heavy fire in the war but he would, from then on, be somewhat callused to the threat of death. He had dodged the bullet, literally, and next time he would accept the very real possibility that it would be his turn to die. His attitude had changed. He would no longer fear death as he had before. In future tight situations others would notice that he didn't appear to be afraid and that could be explained to them by simply saying, "He was at Tarawa."

Holloway and the rest of his battalion left Tarawa on a "liberty ship." These ships were originally mass produced as "emergency ships", constructed quickly and inexpensively for the main purpose of transporting supplies or men. Before the U.S. entered the war a large number of these ships were sent to England to help with their war effort. Because of their utilitarian design they were commonly given nicknames like "ugly duckling." However, when President Roosevelt christened the *Patrick Henry* he ended his speech with the famous quotation of "Give me liberty... or give me death." From then on, they would be known as liberty ships. Each liberty ship seemed to have its own style of cleaving through the water. The waters were rough on this

Prayer before Tarawa landing

Marines going in—Tarawa

"Battle for Tarawa," painting by Sgt. Tom Lovell

Tarawa Charge

Holloway and Elmo Clarke (foreground) headed for the beach.

Tarawa Beach

voyage and the ship's bow would rise up out of the swells, quivering and shaking, then drop to slap the water, only to start rising and trembling again. Of course, Holloway was seasick, having thrown up all he could. The ship was completely loaded and Holloway's unit was the last to get on, so they had to make do on the deck. Holloway found a place on the deck to lie down and sleep. The ocean threw water at him continually and he was soaked, but he slept anyway. This would be his subsistence until they reached Hawaii. But Holloway didn't mind at all. His living conditions had been a lot worse than this. He was leaving Tarawa behind, as much as he could.

After three days at sea, the marines disembarked at Hilo, Hawaii, and were transported to a huge cattle ranch called The Rose Ranch to set up their camp. The Rose Ranch was even larger than the famous Star Ranch in Texas. Located between the active volcanoes of Mauna Kea and Mauna Loa, the ranch spread out for miles and thousands of acres. Here they set to work in groups, first to build tent decks (hundreds of them), then set up the tents, and finally, tent assignments were made. The ground they were camping on was volcanic ash, and the Marines soon noticed that a discarded cigarette butt would burn a hole in the ground as it continued to smolder. As the cigarette would burn, the hole, sometimes several inches across, would just get deeper, becoming a little fire hole. A warning was issued about the fire hazard and the men were told that they would be in big trouble if caught dropping a burning butt. As battalion carpenter, Holloway went to work building tent decks. He was working with Seabee carpenters. The U.S. Navy Construction Battalions (Seabees) were formed at the first of the war to do the construction work wherever they were needed. And they were needed everywhere; where there was fighting, the Seabees were there. The Seabee motto became "We Build; We Fight." Generally recruited for their expertise, many were older than the other Marines and Navy personnel; recruitment ages were from 18 to 60. While on leave they were allowed to wear either a Navy or Marine Corps uniform. Holloway enjoyed working with them. They knew what they were doing, they were hard workers, and they were pleasant to work with. The more Holloway saw of the Seabees, they more he appreciated them.

Once they were settled in, the Marines, as usual, looked for things to do for fun. One diversion was a big rodeo featuring 2nd Division Marines as cowboys and using horses and cattle from the ranch. It was the real thing. The cowboys were ropin' and ridin' and getting launched from the backs of furiously bucking horses. Holloway was amazed at how many bronc-busters there were. The guys whooped and hollered all day.

All other forms of entertainment in Hawaii seemed to involve money. And all the human leeches and con men were there to take as much money as they possibly could from the young Marines. The closest liberty town for the men was Hamakau. (Officers frequented another community with lush facilities for their amusement.) There was a bowling alley, golf course, and bars to keep the men busy. Holloway spent a lot of time in the bowling alley, but also did some golfing and shot pool in the bars. The population of Hawaii at that time was about 85 percent Japanese, and the irony of the situation was not lost on the Marines. For instance, Holloway always felt very nervous getting a haircut from a Japanese woman. When she would start trimming around his ears with a straight razor and he would be leaning back with his neck exposed, Holloway would begin to sweat. He never would have felt that way before the war.

While in Hamakau, Holloway stayed at a small hotel with about 15 rooms run by Mr. & Mrs. Oshima. Although quite rustic, the rooms were kept clean and comfortable by the Japanese couple. And everything was just a short walk away.

One day Holloway was strolling up the street on his way to the bowling alley, thinking of nothing more than the anticipated enjoyment of a little competition with friends. On the way was a favorite bar, and as he got nearer, he could hear a big commotion inside. Holloway looked in and, to his surprise, at the center of the hoopla was a friend of his, Steve "Hoot" Gurnick. Hoot wasn't a very big guy but he was wiry and tough, and, when drunk, he had the delusion that he could whip everyone within shouting distance, all at the same time. He was boisterously announcing that and brandishing a pool cue when Holloway entered. Not surprisingly, there were some Marines anxious to accept the challenge. Luckily for Hoot, two Military Police entered the bar right behind Holloway and the situation was diffused quickly; Holloway had Hoot calmed down and the MPs had everyone else backed off. When Holloway offered to take care of his friend and keep him away from there, the MPs were agreeable. That would save them the bother of having to take him to the brig to sleep it off. Both Holloway and Hoot were staying at the Oshimas' hotel. Hoot was stumbling drunk but he could still ambulate. Holloway walked him back to his room and had to figure out a way to keep him there, so he wrestled his shoes off him and locked them in his own room, leaving the drunk Marine passed out on his bed. The evening was still young, so Holloway headed back downtown. Later that evening Holloway happened to be in the vicinity of that same bar and, déjà vu, he could hear hollering and chairs being thrown around. The shouting sounded like Hoot. Sure enough, as Holloway entered the bar, there was Hoot in his bare feet and in a fighting mood. Hoot took a pool cue and broke it over the edge of the pool table and Holloway yelled at the bartender, "I'll pay for that pool cue!" Just like last time, someone had called the MPs and they magically appeared before anyone got hurt. But this time Holloway couldn't talk them into letting Hoot go back with him. "We've already tried that. This time he's going with us." So off they went. Holloway didn't see his friend for a day or two. When he came back he was the same old Hoot. But his front teeth had been knocked out. He told Stan that he had been treated roughly, but he obviously didn't suffer any ill effects from it, except for the missing front teeth.

One day Holloway walked into his tent to find that someone had stolen his bedroll. So he walked through the camp until he found a quiet, empty tent and he picked up a bedroll off one of the cots and marched off with it. He felt he had no choice. To report something (e.g.- bedroll, helmet, rifle) stolen meant that he would have to pay for another one. When you make $21.00 a month you can't afford to buy very much, especially not expensive supplies. Holloway didn't feel good about stealing another man's equipment, but he felt as if he were caught in a game of musical chairs with bedrolls.

In combat anything could be picked up. Helmets, rifles, and other things could be found strewn about among the corpses. On Tulagi Holloway had found a "Chicago piano," a Thompson sub-machine gun. He immediately found that, when fired, it would rapidly climb straight up. So he got used to holding it sideways. But that machine gun didn't last long—Holloway got tired of having to clean it all the time. So he got rid of it and went back to using his old rifle. In the Solomon islands the Japanese used a 25 caliber rifle, slightly bigger than the common 22, and very accurate. (Holloway took one back to New Zealand and gave it to Robbie) After Guadalcanal the Japanese decided to match the U.S. 30 caliber rifles with weapons firing slightly larger than 30 caliber. That way they could use U.S. ammunition, but U.S. troops couldn't use theirs. That prompted the Japanese to try to steal ammunition instead of blowing it up.

———

Chapter
FIVE

Meanwhile, the war was still raging and the Marines had more islands to invade. They had been resting in Hawaii for seven months and now it was time to leave. When they left, the Marines, of course, had no idea where they would be next. They were on another liberty ship. This one was a "wallower", meaning that it would wallow like a pig in mud to the left, then to the right, to the left, to the right... ad nauseam. Once again, Holloway volunteered for laundry duty, receiving the benefits of that station, which included access to showers and the store whenever he wanted. Probably the best reward for working there was receiving a chit to get you into the mess hall without having to stand in line. This could be a big deal, especially on the smaller, more crowded ships. It was not uncommon to stand in line for one meal, then after eating, go directly to the end of the line for the next meal. You would spend the whole day in line. Holloway always liked the food aboard ship. Even though he was always seasick, he appreciated the quality of the chow, especially compared to what they would be eating in the field.

A little way out of Hawaii they picked up a fleet of ships. There were vessels of all sizes. It was a good feeling to see all those ships and know that the United States had command of the Pacific. The men were finally told that they would be landing on an island called Saipan, in the Marianas Islands, and one step closer to Japan. Where the size of Tarawa was about 1.2 square miles total, Saipan was almost 15 miles long and 7 miles across at its widest point (72 square miles) with a mountain on it.

As usual, the Navy was heavily bombarding the island before the landing. But the Marines had learned not to rely on that to soften the Japanese welcoming committees. What they had come to expect was an enemy fighting force that greatly outnumbered them, and would fight to the death even when defeat was imminent. This time the Marines didn't crawl down the cargo nets. They loaded into the Higgins boats, which were hoisted over the side and lowered into the water. The men were nervous, especially the new replacements. Their stomachs felt turned upside down, and it was difficult to breathe without hyperventilating. In a few short minutes they would be jumping out of the boat and onto the beach where a ferocious Japanese army would be trying to kill them. This is where the sergeants and the corporals took over. They didn't really have to say very much. They had been through Tarawa and they figured that if it was their time to die, so be it. "Let's do it!" Holloway looked over at Sergeant Grivitch. He seemed to be almost serenely calm. Holloway had the utmost respect for Grivitch. He remembered a time when he had been with Grivitch under fire. The sergeant was talking with two other sergeants, standing there like they were at a Sunday picnic, when a Japanese artillery shell exploded nearby. Holloway dove for cover. He looked back over his shoulder and the three sergeants were still standing there chatting as if nothing had happened. That prompted Holloway to get back on his feet very quickly.

The Japanese had let the first wave of Marines onto the island and when they started moving inland the Japanese guns started firing on them. Then they started launching mortars (a short-barreled, high-angled weapon for dropping explosive shells on top of the enemy). When Holloway hit the beach the mortars were dropping out of the sky all over the place. Right in front of them was a very long hill. The Marines that landed before Holloway were slowly working their way up that hill and digging in as they went. Over the hill was an important piece of real estate, the Aslito airfield. The Marines in Holloway's unit laboriously scrambled up the hill, trying to keep a low profile. If you skylined yourself, you were as good as dead. The Marines got used to lying on the ground. If you had to take a pee, you'd simply roll over and relieve yourself. For a while Japanese Zeros were flying in from Tinian Island to either strafe or drop daisy cutters. Also, to add to his displeasure, Holloway worried about the rounds fired from the American ships. With a loud whishing sound, the shells would sail just barely over the Marines' heads. They would joke, "I could reach up and scratch my name on it."

---

155 Seatoun Heights Road
Wellington, E.5.

Letter No. 17 New Zealand
18/6/44

Darling Stan,

Generally I forget to number the letters but I suppose you can fit them in by the dates.

How are things going for you, my darling? I hope you are well and safe but I have an idea that you may be in action and I think of you ever so often.

I've really been a bad girl this week because I didn't write to you about Wednesday as I usually do but there is so little news that I don't know what to tell you.

Monday night I went to a picture party to celebrate the 21st birthday of one of my girlfriends. It was a cold night and we had supper after and there were so many of us that we just about crowded the milk bar out. Tuesday night I stayed home but on Wednesday I went to some plays that an Australian company is putting on at the Opera House. We had to queue up very early to get a decent seat in the gods and there was over an hour to wait before they opened the doors. It was a lot of fun though and when we did get in it was well worth it. The play was a good change from the pictures. Mum and Mary went on Friday and they took some Fish & Chips with them and enjoyed themselves immensely. Going up in the gods reminds Mum of when she used to go up in the gods in the London theatres during the last war. Friday I went to basketball practice and last night I stayed home by the fire.

So you see, Stan, there isn't any news, is there? We haven't heard from Doug since he left Auckland and we are wondering where he is. Mary is writing to him at the moment. Have you got my photo yet? I hope so and don't forget that I'm waiting for one of yours. This is a dreadful letter and if only you were here it would be ever so much better. But, sweetheart, till that time comes this will have to do I suppose.

Meanwhile, please accept lots of love from
Margaret

At one point, the Marines reached a spot where a slight dip in the terrain offered some protection. Despite being pinned down by rifle fire, they were not exposed. About 15 feet from where Holloway dug in were the bodies of four Marines. They had gotten there earlier and had felt pretty relaxed before the mortars started dropping. So relaxed that they had started a little poker game. The mortar had landed right in the middle of their poker game, killing all four instantly. They were sprawled around, one of them still sitting propped against a rock. Another had his arm partly raised, and clutched in his hand was some money, intended to be bet. Cards were scattered around them. The burial detail wouldn't be able to make it up there for maybe a couple of days. Meanwhile the blazing sun beat down on everything, living or dead. There were Marine and Japanese corpses strewn about everywhere. As they bloated in the hot sun the fetid stench of the decay hung over the island so intensely that is was hard to breathe. The only army that wasn't suffering large casualties was the army of flies. They were large black creatures and had seemed to call in reinforcements for a feeding frenzy on the rotting flesh. They were everywhere. Holloway reached over and rapped the butt of his rifle against a big black palm tree. The black surface buzzed and hovered a couple of inches off the tree for just a moment before settling back on it.

Holloway started to unwrap one of the sandwiches that were sent up to them. Waving off the flies, he tried to take a couple of quick bites, hoping he was not devouring some of the swarming insects along with the sandwich. He tried not to think about how those flies had been feasting on dead bodies before they attacked his food.

Just before Holloway moved forward the burial guys appeared and picked up the four dead Marines. One of them noticed the money in the dead clenched hand and Holloway watched as he pried the fingers apart and put the money in his pocket.

Setting up their main bivouac didn't take long. However, there were a number of unexploded shells in the area. The unenviable task of getting them out of camp fell to the munitions man, Mitchell, a friend of Holloway's. Stan watched as Mitchell picked up one of the duds and started to walk away with it under his arm. Something caught his eye—there was smoke trailing out of the shell. "HEY MITCHELL! THAT SHELL'S SMOKIN'!" Picking up his pace, Mitchell hustled to a little gully where he gingerly laid the shell down and let it begin to roll into the ravine. Then he ran like hell. In just a few seconds the shell exploded, harmlessly.

No. 18.
155 Seatoun Heights Rd.
Wellington, E.5.
21st June, 1944

My dearest love,

I hope this finds you well and happy and that you are keeping well away from danger or that danger is keeping well away from you. Since the Invasion of Europe started the War news has been good and maybe if things continue in this good manner it won't be that long before the lights go on again all over the world.

We have had a letter from Doug and he is getting on okay and seems to be quite contented. Of course, everything is novel to him just yet but he says that he has met lots of chaps he knows and that makes a tremendous difference. On Sunday I made quite a discovery. I was speaking to a girl who I have known since I was just knee high to a grasshopper and told her that you were in the 155 mm etc.. and she said she had a friend with the same address. Her friend happens to be Frankie the artist and you can imagine how surprised we both were and how we talked and talked about you two then. Hilda Milestone (that's her name) lives just down the road from us and I have always liked her a lot and Frankie has certainly got a very nice girlfriend. You can tell him that from me but he will know it already.

On Sunday I went to church for the first time in ages and I like going too except that it takes a tremendous effort to make up my mind to go. We won our basketball again on Monday and we are feeling very pleased with ourselves about it. I went up to Aunt Chris and Uncle Maurice's place for tea and they always ask me how you are getting on and are very interested in you. There are lots of people interested in you, as a matter of fact and you are really important, you know.

How's the fan mail going, darling? I suppose you still get tons of letters. I have been getting hardly any from you lately but as I believe you are in action again I shall just have to try and be a little patient. Last night I took Mum to a screening but as it was over early I was in bed by half past 10. Tonight I was home late because I didn't stop work at five o'clock but just went on till half past six. Our shortage of staff is getting acute as this week I've been working so hard that I'm just about worn out at the end of the day. Alan is still swotting very hard and Mary is having her half yearly exams just now. She is reading her history book at the moment.

Well, Stan, it seems that I've about run out of news and the only thing I haven't told you about is the weather.

> *I wonder where you are. I'd love to know but if you are 50 miles away its of as much good as if you are 5000 miles away. Still, this letter may help to bridge the gap between us.*
> *I'll say adieu for now.*
>
> *With lots of love from*
> *Margaret*

A person might not be able to relax very much but, still, you couldn't stay as tight as a wound up spring all the time without breaking, one way or another. Holloway and several other Marines took a few minutes to sit around and have a cup of coffee. As the hot liquid soothingly slid down his throat, Holloway tried to let the knots in his muscles relax a little bit. Sitting with his back against a tree, he thought about how he had gotten used to sleeping in that position. He had slept many nights sitting up, keeping himself and his rifle dry under a poncho in the rain. Just then, the close crack of a sniper's rifle instantly ended any relaxation. Everyone dove for cover. Holloway looked over and saw that one of them hadn't moved. It was Walters, a big southerner who seldom had anything to say. But when he did say something people listened, for everyone knew that Walters was not one to be trifled with. (Once before, Holloway remembered hearing Walters make a meaningful statement. An officer had been haranguing him, and Walters had said, "I think I'll just make it my business to look him up after the war." Holloway had no doubt that he would and that officer would be one very sorry S.O.B.) Walters hadn't been hit. He just sat there and looked at his coffee cup. The sniper's bullet had gone right through it. Coffee was all over his hand and was dripping from what was left of the cup. Walters slowly stood up. "Damn it! You can't even get a cup of coffee!" He threw the cup into the brush, grabbed up his rifle, and trudged away in the direction of the sniper. A short while later Walters found him, hiding out in a cave, and killed him.

Write when ever you can   155 Seatoun Hghts
& as often as you can.   Seatoun E.5.
                              22nd June 1944

Dear Stan

   There have been no letters from you for some
time now, so we are thinking that you must be in
action again. I do hope that you will take all the
care possible of yourself & that God will keep you
safe. It will be a great day when this war is over,
won't it. We will hardly know ourselves. I suppose
Marg has told you that Doug is over that part of
the world where you are Stan, although he may be
quite a way from you. We had the 1st letter from
him last Tuesday, & he says he has met quite a few
boys who he knew in N.Z., also that there are a lot
of Americans there & he was wondering if he would
run across you. Wouldn't it be nice if he did Stan.
My thoughts are with you both all of the time. Marg
is missing you a great deal & it is a red letter
day for her when there is a letter from you. I hope
you are receiving her letters more frequently now
Stan, also that you have her photo by this time. I
have managed to save up enough butter & eggs to make
Doug & you a cake so be on the look out for it.
Mary was saying, that she meant to put the number
of pupil attending her school in the letter she
wrote to you, but forgot to do so. I suppose she
will tell you when next she writes to you. The
weather here this week has been terrible & so cold
& has done nothing but rain. I will be pleased when
the winter is over. I haven't heard from your
Mother again Stan. I do hope she writes to me again,

---

but I know she is very busy & that all of her time must be fully occupied.

Did you get Doug's letter? He wrote it while home on final leave & since then has another address so thought I would give it to you, just in case you have time to write to him, but if you haven't he will quite understand. Here it is

N.Z.436189,
Cpl. Stewart D.H.
A.P.O. 361
Overseas.

There is no news to tell you so will close now May God bless you & keep you safe. I remain

Ever Your friend
Dorothy E. Stewart

There were a lot of caves around and that meant Japs would be hiding in some of them. The Marines had to clear them and be careful while doing it. As Holloway and a few other Marines approached one cave a Japanese soldier stepped out. He was about 50 yards away. Stripped to the waist, he appeared to only have a large knife, which he waved at them in challenge. A friend of Holloway's, Mitchell, had remarked earlier "If I ever get a chance I'd like to take on one of these Japs with a k-bar knife." Now Holloway looked over at Mitchell and saw that his eyes had lit up. He was excited. "I'm going up there with my knife." The others argued with him. They suspected that the guy might have a hand grenade, or just about anything else with which to kill them at close range. Mitchell was nervy; Holloway had been with him for some time and knew he had an abundance of courage. Nobody would change his mind on this matter. This was Mitchell's opportunity to do something he had wanted to do and nobody was going to stop him. Finally, over Mitchell's objections, they shot the Japanese soldier where he stood. They walked up to him and found the knife to be his only weapon. That really made Mitchell mad.

Mitchell was a very likable young man from Iron Mountain, Michigan. His best friend, Mike Aaron, a red-headed boy with a perpetually sunburned nose, hailed from the Michigan town of Sault Ste Marie. They liked to rib each other about which hometown was better. The two Marines were inseparable. Whether it was playing around on leave or taking cover in a foxhole, if you found one, the other would be there too. Unfortunately, the war would soon separate them forever.

Holloway was on guard at the Cossack Post one night when he heard sounds coming from camp. Someone was getting loud. Earlier the Marines had found some left behind saki, and it turned out that one of the men, Frank Murphy, had imbibed just a little bit too much. Murphy didn't just get mean when he was drunk. He got loud. And he would tend to sing Irish songs. That would be fine if Murphy were in some tavern at home. But he was on a small island where people wanted to know exactly where you were so they could kill you. The Marines must have gagged him for a while. But that didn't last. Holloway got a call on the field radio. HQ was upset that he would give away the Marines' position. "He's left camp and he's headed your way. If he makes it up to you, shoot him." "Yes, sir." Holloway could hear him in the distance. He had heard better renditions of "Danny Boy." Holloway wasn't going to shoot him. He might stuff a sock in his mouth and kick his ass back to camp, but he wouldn't shoot him. Fortunately, Murphy passed out before he got that far.

As the Japanese retreated the Marines found souvenirs left behind. One of them was a 50-powered glass with night vision. Holloway used it while on watch. One night he heard movement and used the glass to find out what it was. What he saw was a dog. The poor thing was wandering around trying to stay alive, but too apprehensive to come into the Marine camp. Other things captured from the Japanese as they pushed them across the island included lots of Japanese money and a phonograph with records. They used the money for playing poker, and it was not uncommon to hear "I'll raise you a million yen!" Sometimes they would play the Japanese music, but it sounded so strange to them—shrill and squeaky. They still had fun with it. A battle-weary Marine would walk into camp, heavy stubble on his face, covered with island dirt and grime, and say to another tired-looking Marine "May I have the honor of this next dance?" The other Marine, cigarette hanging out of his mouth, would shift his eyes to look at him and respond "Nothing would please me more, but it seems my dance card is full."

Letter No. 19
155 Seatoun Heights Rd.
Wellington, E.5.
25th June, 1944

Dearest Stan,

Mary has a girlfriend staying for the weekend so I have given my bed up and am sleeping on one of the camp beds in the sitting room. It's very uncomfortable and freezing cold and reminds me of the time you slept here in exactly the same place only you didn't say that it was uncomfortable though I suppose it was. I thought of you last night until I went to sleep. I haven't heard from you this last week but I'm sure that you are giving me a thought or two. I hope you are anyhow and I realise that if you are in action it is impossible for you to write.

It's hard to concentrate on this as there are several disturbing elements: the wireless is on and Mary and her girlfriend are giggling and Mum and Dad are talking. But it takes more than a bit of noise to stop me from writing to you. There could be thunder and lightning but I wouldn't care.

Mum has made you a cake and we will be posting it to you this week. I hope you enjoy it, Stan. The last one had some whiskey on it to preserve it but I suppose this one will keep well enough until it reaches you. It has been a sunny day today though cold in the shade and I have been outside most of the time trying to pull a few weeds out. The part I enjoy most of gardening is picking the flowers and I love doing that. Friday I went to basketball practice as usual and then went to the pictures. I have not been to the A.N.A. for weeks and weeks and now have lost all desire to go. These cold nights make me feel like staying home and once I'm here in front of the fire it is hard to budge. Old Nigel finds it hard too and lies almost on top of it. He uses the hearth as a pillow and his little paws are folded up. He's such a dear I'd like to hug him right now. I'd like to hug you too but you are miles away and probably you have a beard a couple of feet long by now. Have you? And I suppose you have a lovely tan too.

Last night I went down to the Seamen's Mission and danced with some English boys who are in port for a couple of days. Sometimes they have such an accent that I can hardly understand what they are speaking about. It's almost like a foreign language and I remember

I had the same difficulty with some of the American accents. Still the important American was very easy to understand and he has such a lovely deep voice it's a thrill just to listen to it and wouldn't it be wonderful if the 'phone rang and that voice said "Is that you Marg?" I hope the day is not far distant when I'll hear you speaking to me again, Stan.

Meanwhile it's time I said 'adieu' so

Lots of love and kisses from
Margaret

First Sergeant Burhaugh was a shotgun man. He had found that flushing the enemy from the caves and other tight hiding places sometimes required close up fighting and the shotgun was just the tool for it. He didn't carry an M-1 or a machine gun, but he always carried a shotgun. It was Burhaugh who spotted the dugout. He and Holloway were out together looking for dug-in enemy. On one end of the dugout was a slot, large enough to look in or out and the two Marines very cautiously peered in. What they saw was a group of about twenty people, lying around either asleep or pretending to be. There was one man in a Japanese uniform, but the rest looked like civilians, probably some of the Chinese and Koreans who had been brought to Saipan to work for the Japanese. They looked done in. Who could blame them, after surviving a massive bombardment of the island, and being caught in the middle of the island assault. Burhaugh said, "I'm going in," and he quietly walked around to the door at the other end. Holloway could see everyone in the dugout, as he aimed his rifle through the slot. If there were any move to raise a weapon, he would nail it. Burhaugh opened the door and slowly walked in with his shotgun raised. He reached out and put his hand on the shoulder of an old woman, shaking her awake. Once he had her attention, he tried to tell her, through sign language, to come with him and they would be fed. The old woman got up and started moving around. She was looking for food—she was going to feed Burhaugh. Apparently that's what he was asking for. Burhaugh and Holloway had no problem getting them back to camp. It was a blessing for them to be found, and to still be alive.

In camp was Gunnery Sergeant Garvin, a 30-year man. Garvin was well respected. He had served his time in different hot spots over the years and was well acquainted with combat. On this day he had no idea that he was about to renew an old friendship from years past. One of the prisoners was calling his name. He had a Japanese uniform on but he was Chinese. Garvin recognized him; he had been his servant while he was stationed in China. Here they were reunited in the least likely of places, under the grimmest of circumstances. They were both very happy to see each other. After they were fed, the other people in the group were taken to a prison compound on another part of the island. But Garvin's friend stayed in camp. Garvin made sure that his friend was well taken care of. He let it be known to the other Marines that this was a close personal friend of his and if he wasn't treated like a gentleman someone would be answering to Garvin.

To clean up around the camp the men built a big fire and began to throw trash and other burnables on it. Holloway gathered up some garbage and tossed it into the flames, then walked toward the perimeter to pick up some more refuse. BOOM! Someone had stoked the fire with a pile of stuff that included a Japanese concussion grenade, one that threw less shrapnel but was loud and disorienting. Several Marines were close enough to be wounded, but not seriously, and they were hustled off to the infirmary. Right away, word came down to the outfit that those wounded in that episode would not be receiving purple hearts, a medal awarded to those wounded in combat. That announcement provoked a lot of cussing and complaining but there was nothing they could do about it.

155 Seatoun Heights Road.
Wellington, E.5.
29th June, 1944

My dearest Stan,

I wonder where you are and I hope this letter finds you well and happy. I feel sure that you must be in action now and please take care and look after yourself.

I really haven't much to write about because I have no news to tell you. Life goes on and one day is very much like the next. If there happens to be a letter that makes the day a red-letter one but it's exactly three weeks ago that I last heard from you and it's also three weeks since Hilda heard from Frankie.

Anyhow, Stan, we do know that Doug is at Bougainville and our curiosity is satisfied on that score. He says that lots of the boys can't take the heat but he is weathering it okay. He has met quite a number of fellows he knows and our cousin who lives in Auckland went to Bougainville at the same time as Doug. My cousin is the chief meteorologist officer in those Islands and holds quite a high rank so I don't suppose Doug will have that much to do with him.

We played basketball on Monday and won again so that we are now top in our grade. I hope we keep the good work up. Tuesday night I went to the pictures at the local theatre and it's only the second time in my life that I've ever been by myself. I didn't decide to go till the last minute but Dad has a week off work this week and has been drunk every day and as he was playing up on Tuesday night I thought it better to go out than stay at home. At a certain point you feel that you'll either go mad or have to get out.

Mary and Alan are in the middle of exams just now. Mary seems to have grown up ever such a lot in the past few weeks and I guarantee she'll have all the boys on the run in a year or two. She is still as funny as ever and should really have been a comedian.

Do you like strawberries? I do too and this next weekend I'm planting some down the back so by next Christmas we should be having strawberries but, alas, no cream because of rationing. I am also putting in a daphne plant and a boronia. It's a native of Australia and has the most beautiful smell. How is your mother's garden Stan, or doesn't she get enough time to do anything in it now?

Do you have films where you are? Doug says they have about 3 a week but surely you are not that much in the jungle. But I should use the past tense there, shouldn't I. Because you can't be in your rest camp now? I must say that this letter is about as cheerful as a funeral march but, you know, I never have been much of a writer. Tonight I'm off to one of my girlfriend's place. Her name is Dorothy and she is getting married shortly and tonight I'm going to see *her trousseau and going away clothes. In fact I'm going to see everything and we'll talk of nothing but weddings. I'm still waiting for that photo of my beloved so don't forget it, will you?*

I shall sign off now and with this goes miles and miles of love. Of course, one can't measure love by miles or anything else though love is such a big thing.

From your ever loving
Margaret

Saipan was a harsh island. There were some trees and lots of rocks. The Japanese had brought over goats to graze on the countryside. That was about all you could do with the land. Goats were everywhere. With them clattering around on the island, the Marines were kept in a nervous state, not knowing if the movement was the enemy about to open fire on them or just a goat. Holloway was jittery anyway. He was sitting under a large tree one night with a small group of Marines around him. They had been assigned to a Cossack post at the top of a rise about four miles from camp. Holloway always felt more secure in the daylight where he could see what was happening. In the dark the enemy could sneak up on their position without being detected. He looked to his left at a nearby cane field and thought how easy it would be for a Jap to crawl up close and lob a grenade into them. Suddenly, as if his thoughts had willed it to happen, he heard it come crashing down through the branches above him. All the men desperately scrambled and dove for cover. It hit the ground with a loud thump, but it didn't explode. There was silence as they waited for the concussion and flying shrapnel. But it didn't come. Maybe it was a dud. They couldn't leave a live grenade in the middle of their outpost; they had to find it. Holloway crawled back to the tree and began to feel around in the dark. His fingers lightly bumped against it and his automatic response was to flinch back. Then he extended his arm and laid his hand on it. He would have to pick the grenade up and throw it and hope it wouldn't blow away part of his body. But it felt different. It wasn't metallic; it was big; it was a breadfruit. Holloway nervously laughed, then sat up and announced in a stage whisper, "False alarm! It's a breadfruit!"

In the daylight, Holloway looked over at a nearby hillside with some goats ambling across it. "If I could catch one of these goats, I'd milk it," he said to the men around him. After all, he was an old farm boy. Within fifteen minutes some Marines had grabbed a goat and dragged it over to him. Holloway plopped his helmet on the ground, sat on it, and started milking. He squirted the milk into another helmet and continued to squeeze away until the goat was dry. Several of the men sampled it. It wasn't bad. The next issue that came out of the Marine Corps magazine, "The Leatherneck", had a drawing on the front cover of a Marine milking a goat. It had to be Holloway.

As the Marines pushed on, the Japanese became more desperate. They were being pushed down toward the far end of the island. The Marines were aware that the Japanese, when facing defeat, would probably resort to a banzai attack. That meant an all out suicide attack. They had seen this on Guadalcanal and Tarawa. If the Japanese Emperor himself ordered the attack it was called "Gyokusai", or "Death with honor." The battle cry was "Seven lives for the Emperor!" which meant that in dying the Japanese soldier was to take seven Americans with him. No one knows for sure if the Emperor himself ordered the attack, but it became clear that the Japanese soldiers believed he had. The two commanders, Lt. Gen. Yoshitsugu Saito and Vice Admiral Chuichi Nagumo, organized the suicide assault then went back to their quarters and killed themselves in the traditional Japanese way—they disemboweled themselves and were finished off with a pistol shot to the head from their aides. It started off as an organized assault on the American perimeter, and became a broiling mass of Japanese humanity, running and screaming into and over the soldiers on the perimeter. The Japanese had been given sake just prior to the assault, and some charged in a drunken stupor. But all continued to move forward with the thought of killing the American enemy and dying an honorable death.[1]

———

Holloway could hear them coming, several thousand Japanese soldiers all screaming together. Then he saw them coming. They had broken through the lines and were advancing at a steady if not brisk pace. Leading the charge were two tanks and the Japanese soldiers used them for cover as they advanced. By this time the Marine artillery guns had been lowered down so that they were shooting level at the oncoming Japs. The Marines were shooting at the charging enemy as fast as they could but in a few minutes they would be having to deal with hordes of demented and/or drunk soldiers shooting at them at point blank range and trying to cut them into pieces with samurai swords. Holloway wondered "Is this going to be the end? If it is, I won't go easy." He glanced over to his right and saw a Marine hustle by and step off into the brush. He carried a large tube on his shoulder. It was a bazooka. Holloway had never seen one in action before. The next thing he knew, he heard a loud whoosh and one of the Japanese tanks exploded. Then another whoosh and the other tank exploded. With the two tanks blowing up in front of them, the Japanese soldiers lost some of their steam. They continued to advance, but now they were exposed, out in the open, and the big artillery guns were firing almost point blank at them. A few still got through and into the artillery, but the Japanese surge had been stopped. The bazooka had turned the tide and the Marines quashed the final banzai attack on Saipan.

[1] *Reader's Digest Illustrated Story of World War II*, The Reader's Digest Association, Inc., 1978, pp. 442-450.

The Gyokusai was over. Thousands of Japanese soldiers had died on that one day, July 7, 1944. In front of the artillery was a field of jumbled blood, and guts, and body parts. The Japanese would continue to fight, but their organized resistance had been severely crippled.

Holloway's unit set up a Cossack Post on the main trail to try to keep the area clear of enemy. They rigged booby traps, trip-wired with hand grenades.There were still Japanese everywhere and the Marines were on edge, expecting to bump into the enemy at any time. While on watch, Holloway and two other Marines were standing, talking together when a Japanese soldier walked out of the brush just a few feet from them. All three Marines shot at the same time, killing him instantly.

At night at the Cossack post the men would sleep in a row, close enough to touch those lying beside them. One of them would stay awake, on watch, and when his watch was over he would wake up the man next to him to take over. One night one of the men, Wilson, was in pain, and kept groaning loudly enough that they feared he might give away their position to the enemy. They couldn't get him back to camp—it was four miles away, and it was pitch dark.

Wilson was about 18 years old with rounded features. He looked as if he were packing some extra fat—a little bit rotund. But his appearance was deceiving. Being out of shape and being a Marine were mutually exclusive terms. Wilson could keep up with everyone else. He was well liked; Holloway thought he was a nice kid. As the others slept on a large mound of solid rock and a little bit of dirt, Holloway kept his eyes peeled and his nerves on alert watching for any movement in the night. Things were quiet except for Wilson's continual groans. Near the end of his shift Holloway crawled over to Wilson's sack and laid his hand on the kid's forehead. He was hot. Holloway put a wet rag on his brow—that was all he could do for now. In the morning they would see about getting him to the infirmary. Holloway crawled back to his sack, woke the next guy for watch, and went to sleep. At daylight, as Holloway was waking up, he heard someone say, "Wilson's dead." Sure enough, he was lying there cold and still with his eyes closed. They would never know what killed him.

155 Seatoun Hghts
Seatoun E.5.
Wellington
4th July 1944

My Dear Stan

I see by the papers that you are in the thick of the fighting again, & my thoughts & prayers are for you, & I do pray that God will keep you safe. Margaret is worrying about you & wondering how you are & is longing for a letter from you, so I do hope it will not be long before she hears from you. I think that you boys of the 2nd Marines have done more than your share of the fighting & it is about time that you had a spell from it. We have not heard from your Mother lately & trust she is well. Marg had a very nice letter from your brother Norman on Saturday & I think he must be like his brother Stan, a very nice boy. Yesterday we had a letter from Doug who I think is at Bougainville & he says he has been on the look out for you. He is in the canteen, so if ever you are there you can look him up. Just now, it is bitterly cold & the other day we had a slight sprinkling of snow. The children were wishing that it would settle & snow real hard, so that they could have a snow fight, & to tell you the truth, I wouldn't mind one myself. It would remind me of home a great deal & of the snow fights I used to have with my brothers. It was quite nice until one went down ones neck & then it wasn't so nice.

Well Stan, today is Independence day, but what a way for you boys out there to spend it, but never mind, here's hoping that next year you will be in your own homes with the ones you love & that your dreams will come true. You know what I mean Stan. We are all well here. Mary & Alan are in the middle of exams, so are busy swotting. Last night Marg played basketball, but her team lost the game. Up until then they were leading in the class, so I suppose they will be second now. The other week Marg's name was mentioned in the sports paper here, as she was scoring so many goals, so I suppose she must be quite good. Tonight Marg, Mary & I are going to see a play that is on at the Opera house. I wish you were here to come with us Stan.

Have you got Marg's photo yet? I do hope you got it before going into action, as I know you were looking forward to receiving it. There is no more news to tell you, so will close now. Write whenever you can & take care of yourself Stan, & may God bless you.

Ever your friend
Dorothy E. Stewart

Eventually, the Japanese were pushed to the northern end of the island where there were very high cliffs. Many chose to jump off the cliffs, landing on the rocks below, instead of surrender. Some of them were civilians. They had been told that the Americans were ruthless savages who would do all kinds of torturous things to them before killing them. No amount of pleading over loud speakers could dissuade them. Women threw their babies over and then jumped after them. It was a grim and horrible mass suicide.

The killing and dying on Saipan gradually came to an end. The Marines settled into work details. Holloway found himself helping to load equipment and wounded onto a barge. The sun was blazing down, as usual. Holloway looked over at the clear blue water. It seemed to be beckoning him and he wasn't going to resist. Already shirtless, he kicked off his boots and dove in. How refreshing! When he came up he was about thirty feet from the barge and moving fast. There was a strong current, like a river, carrying him away. He was going past the end of the ship when someone threw him a line and dragged him out. In their outfit was a champion swimmer by the name of Sabo, who immediately saw this as a challenge that he would accept. Man against current. Into the water he went and he swam like a demon. But the current was too much and they had to throw him a line too.

"Marines hug beach on first day, Saipan June 1944"   *Cpl.J. Glozak*

"SWING SHIFT—it appears that one Marine is relieving another on the beach at Saipan but they are really crawling, under enemy fire, to their assigned positions. Saipan June, 1944"

Sgt. James Burns

"Surrendering—dazed momentarily by shell fire, this Jap leaves his cave at an unsteady gait. The Marine thinks the Jap will surrender and witholds his fire but the Marine does not see a stick of dynamite the Jap has clutched in his right hand."

"ROUTING THEM OUT -A Marine with a flame thrower routes out Japs from their cave strongholds at the northern end of the island during the final fighting of Saipan. The buildingin front of the caves also felt the torch of the flame throwers. Saipan 12 July, 44"

"Marine throws grenade at Japs in cave on Saipan"

"This Jap soldier resisted capture, tried Hari Kari and made himself generally a nuisance, even after he was assured that he would not be mistreated so he was brought into the proper authorities in this ungraceful manner. June 23, 1944 Saipan"

Pfc. Horace A Smith

"Dead Jap and destroyed tank on Saipan"

"16 inch dud."

H&S Bat 2nd 155 mm. Arty. Bn.(How)
Corps Artillery V.A.C.
c/o Fleet P.O. San Francisco, Calif.
July 14, 1944

My Darling,

It's so long since I've written to you I suppose you think I've forgotten you, but surely you have more faith than that. The truth is I am on Saipan and have been here from the first so haven't been able to write. I really believe it's been harder on me than you. I can't tell you much about this push. No doubt you can find out much more from the papers.

I've missed you terribly, dearest, and think of you continually. Your letters have been coming thru wonderfully, and they sure boost my morale. The last was dated June 12th. I'm sorry if I sound down hearted in my letters. I suppose you think a guy should be happy when he gets "no" for an answer. You said "what difference does it make as we couldn't see each other until after the war anyway. It only means the difference between living and existing or the difference between planning or being dormant. Nevertheless I expected just such an answer so am not too deeply hurt nor surprised. You still rate first with me.

Darling, you forgot to tell me how much too large the ring was, also to tell me all your sizes. How do you expect me to pick out nice things for you when I get home if I don't know your size? I'll not forget you Marg.

V.A.C. means fifth Amphibious Corps. And I'm afraid I can't answer all the other questions. Tell your Mum I will write to her. She writes very nice letters and always tells me the things I want to know. Your photo hasn't arrived yet. I guess it is in the Marine art gallery. Would you please send me another. Mom got one and said it was a darling. I'll cut that part of her letter out and send to you. I would send the whole letter but am afraid it would run over weight for air-mail. Mom said she put your photo next to mine on the piano. I hope you don't mind your photo keeping company with mine.

I'm sorry Doug was shipped out. I hope everything goes well with him as my best wishes for good luck do. I hope it isn't too hard for your Mum. If I should meet him I'm sure it would be a pleasant meeting. If he ever gets on the same island with me

I'm sure I'll be able to find him. God grant that he may return to you soon.

In one of your letters you said you was blue and might someday tell me why. I don't understand why you didn't tell me then. I don't want you to be blue, and although I have no right to ask reason for your moods, I think you would find me a most sympathetic confidant, and perhaps I could help you. I had hoped I could make your troubles mine but now I'm bothering you with my heart again. I'm glad that you have done well in basketball. You excel in quite a number of things Marg. Guess you'll always be first with me. Mom would be hurt if she knew I was writing to you before I do her or anyone on this first opportunity to write. I haven't heard from Sis in a long time. Guess she has forgotten me. Yet I know she wouldn't. Wally and Sponcey are both still in the States. I've had no word from Gerry, but still think I'll win that bet. He hasn't forgotten you darling. Don't feel too bad. Well there's only one of you darling and that is You so take care of yourself and remember me as

Your Loving
Stan

Finally, it was time to leave Saipan. Holloway didn't have any idea where he would be going next, but he wanted to put the stench and horror of Saipan permanently behind him. Tarawa was a horrible experience, but it had lasted about three days; Saipan had taken almost a month. The ship that would take them away from there was the big, beautiful *Monrovia*. When Holloway boarded the ship he had very few possessions—few clothes, no towel, no sheets or blankets. A sailor walked up to him and handed him a towel. Imprinted on the towel was the sailor's name—"Farr." So Holloway took his towel and showered, then reported for work at the laundry. For many years Holloway would keep that towel and he would always remember the sailor, Farr, and his compassionate gesture that meant so much to a very weary Marine.

The Navy guns had bombarded the island of Guam for 17 days before the Marines stormed the island on July 21, 1944. The Americans had been looking forward to taking the island back ever since the 153-man Marine garrison there had surrendered to the Japanese on December 10, 1941. At first, resistance at the two beach landing zones had been vicious. However, by the time Holloway's unit landed the resistance had been broken. The first thing the Colonel ordered was for Sergeant Grivitch to take a squad of about 35 men, locate the enemy, and engage them if necessary. They wanted to know where the Japanese were and what they were doing. Holloway and Grivitch stuck together. Wherever Grivitch went Holloway made sure he went too, and when Grivitch selected men for these missions he always took Holloway. The sergeant reminded Holloway of a bulldog, with a strong jaw, no-nonsense look about him. He was tough and smart, with lots of courage. People remark about others with the highest accolade, "If I were in combat, I would want him with me." Well, Holloway had been and was in combat and he knew exactly who he wanted with him. Grivitch also had a rare talent as a cartographer. Holloway could pinpoint spots with an aiming circle and the sergeant would make an accurate map with them.

Guam had had some farms mixed in with the small trees and lots of brush. The Navy bombardment had knocked down fences and barns, leaving livestock scattered and wandering on the island. One hundred miles south of Saipan, Guam was ten miles longer, five miles wider, and three times larger. The brush was thick enough in places that you could walk right by the enemy and not even know it. On that mission, the Japanese stayed well away from them. The Marines cautiously traversed through the foliage, across the island, until they reached the other shore. No enemy to be found. What that told them was that the Japanese were on the run.

H&S Bat, 2nd 155 mm. Arty Bn.(How)
Corps Artillery V.A.C.
c/o Fleet P.O. San Francisco, Calif.
July 27, 1944

My Dearest,

I will take this opportunity to tell you I am on Guam and am well. Doug and I are still a good way apart. I would like to see him. For a time it will be impossible to write to anyone but you, Aunt Mildred and Mother. Please tell everyone I will write to them when I can and I hope they will be patient with me and keep writing. Mom wrote and said Calla's little girl had fallen from a swing or something and was hurt quite seriously but is improving and she is going to be OK. She had a cracked pelvis and several other injuries. Calla's little boy has the whooping cough but is doing alright now. Her husband is hoping to get a commission in the Navy. She seldom writes anymore. Mom gives me all the family news. I'll say you was wrong when you said Hawaii was about the best Pacific Island. That's where I was stationed before I came out here. I have seen but few places I disliked as much as Hawaii and hope I never go back there, but I would like to see N.Z. again. I went to Entiwetok then Saipan now here. I've been getting around a little and would like to go home or to N.Z. after this is over. I hardly think there is much chance of that though.

I still haven't got the photo yet Darling. I hope you'll send another. I haven't got either of the cakes as yet but am sure they'll be good. I suppose you have the pictures Mom sent you by now.

Tell me which ones they were and if they aren't terrible will you? I don't recall Mom having any good pictures of me. Aunt Mildred has most of them. Elsie has some pictures left there too.

Well Marg I'm in hopes it wont be too long now before this is over and I can start to live again. There would be no future in here for me in peace time. I had better bring this to a close now hoping this finds you and yours all enjoying the best in health and happiness.

Love
Stan

GARDNER FIELD
TAFT CALIFORNIA

8/1/44
Gardner Field
Taft, Calif.

Dear Marg,

I'll bet this is sure a big surprise to you, but Stan has told me so much about you, and all he told me was good. He said I ought to write to you so, as you can see, that is what I am doing.

It is rather hard to write to someone you don't know, so I guess I'll start out by telling you about myself. I am in the "Air Corps" and stationed at Gardner Field, California. Stan always told me never to join but I did anyway and now I realize just *what he meant. I really like it if it weren't for so much time wasted. I would like to get thru with this course and get to do something and try to accomplish something.*

I am now an Aviation Student and I don't fly yet but should start flying in Sept. or Oct. Now all I get to do is pre-flight them and start them and taxi them around. I'm crazy about flying and have always been. I am really praying that I can make the grade because I'm afraid I will be awful disappointed if I don't.

We have a darn stiff course here it is 13 hours a day one week, and 15 hours a day the next. Our physical training course is the worst of them all. It consists of running a 3 mile course, calisthenics and a lot more physical activities. We have 6 hours a week of this and 6 hours a week of drill, then we have "On the Line Training" 9 hours a day. On the line training is just working on planes and getting familiar with them. We have BT-13A's at this field. They are the little planes pictured at the top of this page.

Our chances of graduating and getting our commissions are very small, because they have an over supply of pilots. So far I have done swell but you never can tell what can happen. They are so strict on discipline that you can't even have any dust on your equipment or they "gig" you, or even wash you out.

Well Marg, That's about all I have to tell about myself. So I will close hoping I will hear from you and tell me all about New Zealand and yourself. I will let my wife write some in this same letter.

A Friend
Wally

Amity, Ore. U.S.A.
Aug. 6, 1944

Dear Mrs. Stewart and Margaret,

You have been long neglected but I wanted to get a letter from Stan before I answered so I might hear both sides before I answered your letters. You know he has been in battle again so mail came slowly. Poor kid, it seems as if he has drawn a hard lot—seems as if he gets into most of the real hard battles and he is so blue it makes my heart ache. I love you Margaret because my boy does and because you seem so good and sensible. This letter is hard to write but in no way do I mean to hurt you. If you did not love Stan more than anyone else you did right to "turn him down" as he says. Yet it has been hard on him for there are as he says, "no hopes, no dreams, no happy plans, only the horrors of battle." Yet as I told him better that than to have you both miserable later. Stan's country is the good old U.S.A. Would you be happy with him here? Stan is a farmer. Would you like that life? If he were wounded would you want him anyway? These are some questions you must answer for yourself. If you care enough, tell him and help him to have you to dream about and your home, now when he needs you so badly but if you don't love him enough don't keep him dangling. It makes him too miserable.

Please don't be angry, I am only trying to tell you as I would Calla. I want you happy if you should come here—and I would do anything to make you that way. Don't you feel that way, Mrs. Stewart? I know you would hate to lose your girl but with planes etc. she could go home. I almost hated my son-in-law when he took my only daughter away but I'm glad I didn't say anything against it, for they are truly happy even if I've not seen her for four long years and have never seen my grand children— and they're darlings too from their pictures.

Don't do as I say, Margaret look into your heart and do as it says.

It's been terribly hot here 104 degrees and that is very warm for Oregon, the air is so humid and depressing when the mercury climbs so high. Amity is only a small village and Farmington is smaller. I like Amity tho' it's quiet but anything but dead. We go to McMinnville (8 miles away) for all our picture shows or to Portland for trading or later shows.

Oregon is a beautiful state. It never gets very cold here but it rains a good deal in winter and Stan hates that. Stan is a great boy to love to go here and there for week end trips or vacations. We think we will build us a cabin on the beach so any of the kiddies can have it when they want a change. The firs are grand, so are the flowers, lakes, & the mountains. I love Oregon.

Well, it's nearly school time again. My school board raised me $30.00 a month over last year. I'll get $1,620.00 for nine months this year. That's $180.00 a month or $9.00 a day. The government taxes that heavily though so I'll only get about $153.00 a month for myself. We are having our house remodeled. We have a new porch in front and the roof re-shingled. We are going to paint it white. We are also building a garage.

Wally and June are in California now. Wally wants to write to you so I sent him your address. June works in Safeway store at Taft so she can be near him. He is in the air corps you know. The war looks good right now. I do so hope it will be over.

The gardens and flowers are drying up and still we should expect that at this time of year. My chrysanthemums are growing nicely and I hope they do well.

Dad and I sang at a funeral this afternoon. I didn't know the man who was buried. We have a new minister at our church. We like him very much. I teach the adult class in Sunday School and get a lot of kick out of it. I am also choir director and am proud of my choir. They sing very nicely together. Gas is so short that we all stay home rather closely. Butter, milk, cheese and meat take red ration points and it really takes lots of planning to make them go around.

Good night, dear friends, its bed time. Write again soon. I'll try to answer sooner.

Love
Leda M. Holloway

Fort Lewis Wash
Sunday, Aug. 27, 1944

Hello Marg,

I received your very nice letter yesterday and was very glad to hear from you and your letter was very interesting. I really haven't very much to say because when it comes to letter writing I am no good.

Thank you very much for the pictures of Wellington. And they are very exciting.

You asked me about Chinese in Frisco. Well there is a very few of them here but almost every town on the west coast has a place in it called China Town and almost all of the people who live there are Chinese. I am sorry that I don't have some pictures of Oregon or Portland. I never did care very much for San Francisco.

Excuse me for writing on the back of the paper but I am almost out of paper right now.

I am all through with my training in San Francisco and I am now at Fort Lewis Washington. It is about 40 miles south of Seattle and about 450 miles southwest of Spokane and it is about 200 miles from home.

You said that we must be a smart family. Well I tell you Stan and Calla was very smart in school but Wally and I were the dumbest kids on earth but we always had a way with our teachers so we would pass alright. Say talking of being smart you seemed to be not bad. When your brother comes 8th out of 180.

Say Marg I am very glad that you think a little of Stan because that guy is sure a swell kid and he is about the hardest worker that you ever saw. Stan and I used to have some good *times together and we used to work in Farmington Washington together and we used to really enjoy ourselves. He used to lose his temper when the tractor wouldn't go or something.*

I don't have a good picture of myself but I will send you one of me and my best friend who was my friend at home. His name is Bruce Williams, in the army air corps, and he used to work in Wash with Stan and I.

You asked me if I like to play snooker and billiards. Well I don't know very much about them but I do play some pool. Someday maybe you can come to the U.S. and see all what we have and after the war I am planning on coming to New Zealand just to see your country and see you and maybe I can shoot some wild hogs. Stan told me all about his hogs hunting and he said that it is lots of fun. You ask me about Oregon called the Webb (sic) foot state, you are right. It is called that because of its rain but it isn't so bad. And Oregon has more trees that any State in the U.S.

I am sorry but I must close for now.

Best Wishes
Sponcy

P.S. Be good and don't work to (sic) hard

H&S Btry, 2nd 155 mm. Howitzer Bn
c/o Fleet PO San Francisco, Calif.
October 20, 1944

Dearest Mom and Dad,

I'm too happy to write a run-of-the-mill letter tonight, but I have to write and tell you all this good news. Marg has promised to come home to marry me after the war. I wish it could be sooner and I have a plan which I have suggested to her and if she will consent I'm going to ask you to help to get her there so she'll be there when I come home. She has written to you telling you all about it, but I don't suppose you have her letter yet. Save that letter or send it to me. Folks I don't deserve such a fine wife but God knows I'll try to be worthy of her. I never thought I could win, but now that I have I'll always be thankful. You will both love her I'm sure. You can't help but see she is class.

Do you think I'll be able to find a way to support her after I get out? I don't think I can count on farming for Aunt M. She's not going to like this arrangement I'm afraid so I'll have to make it on my own. I'm sure I can make a go of it. Will you mind if I can get Marg to come to you so she will be there when I come home and As soon as her father finds out he will cut her off without a cent which suits me to a T. He has other plans for his daughter, but this is not true with Mum. She'll be on our side. I will make arrangements to support Marg from the time she leaves home until I can marry her then I'll take over dual responsibilities and if we have our way it won't be too long until I'll have tri-responsibilities, etc.

Did you get the good picture of Marg I sent to you and do you like it? It's just like her. That other picture was terrible wasn't it? You'll both get a kick out of the way she talks and the perfect English she uses. She is quite different from most the girls we used to bring home. Marg is quiet-mannered never swears or drinks. She'll need a little schooling on cooking though I'm sure you'd help her at that wouldn't you Mom? She can cook but not all the good things you can by a long shot.

Tell Dot I'll write to her right soon. I got a real nice Xmas pkg from her and a nice letter. She certainly knows how to write interesting letters. I guess that's about all folks. Write real soon and tell me what you think. I'll close for now hoping you are both well and happy as I am.

Your Son
Stan

"Tanks blasting Jap pillboxes as Marines crouch for cover. Snipers very active.

*Guam
August,1944"*

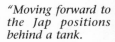

"Moving forward to the Jap positions behind a tank.

*Guam
Sgt. R. Robbins
July 1944"*

*"They dig in for the night while their buddy offers protection for them...
These Marines know how important a fox-hole is even when you are sleeping.*

Guam July 1944 Sarno"

"BURNING THE ENEMY OUT—Marines turned away from the intense heat, when they used a flame thrower to drive the enemy from a building on Guam. The Japs who lived dashed out a rear door and were shot down by other Leathernecks using automatic rifles.

Aug 3, 1944 Cpl. A. J. Curry"

WRONG PASSWORD—Marine corporal Chester S. Cooper of Tulsa, Okla. examines a dead Japanese soldier who attempted to pass through the American lines on Guam during the night. Cooper challenged him and when he received the wrong password the Marine took no chances and opened fire. The Leathernecks were asleep not five yards for [sic] the scene."

PACIFIC WAR MARINE

Chapter
SIX

T he Japanese had not been friendly to the people on Guam since capturing the island. Holloway came across an American woman with two Japanese children, one walking beside her and the other being carried on her hip. She told of the Japanese killing her husband and the other men, and of how they abused her. She had endured and seen a lot, her scars were deep, and she had an intense hatred for the Japanese.

On Guam the Marines did encounter bitter fighting taking Mount Alifan and the Orote Peninsula. Holloway assisted in pinpointing positions for the big 155 howitzers, which could throw a 95 pound projectile. Luckily, he didn't get any closer to the fighting. A counterattack was launched by the Japanese, loaded up with sake, but was overcome by the Marines. Finally, the Marines captured Orote airfield and sounded "To the Colors" on a captured Japanese bugle to announce the raising of the American flag on the battle ravaged parade ground for the first time since December 10, 1941.

When Guam was secured, the Marines were told to board ship. There were other stepping stones of islands to assault, but for now they would be headed back to Hawaii.

It was nice to be back at the old familiar digs of Camp Tarawa. The Marines set up their tents on the same platforms that Holloway had previously helped build. It was just like a town with streets, albeit only for walking. Holloway felt as if he were rooming in luxury, in a nice, clean tent with a cot to sleep on, and shared with five other men.

It was early February of 1945 that Stan's old friend, Jerry Howery, found Holloway at Camp Tarawa. Howery had recovered from malaria and had been assigned to another unit. Awaiting his orders in Hawaii, he found out that Holloway was there, too. Holloway was delighted to see Howery. Last time he'd seen him, Howery's pallor had been the color of white paste; he'd been a sick hombre. But now, shaking hands with him, Jerry looked the picture of health. After saying hello to the others, (Martin was there, as well as another close friend of Stan's, a handsome, dark, round-faced Californian by the name of John P. Soares) Howery sat down on Holloway's cot and they started filling in the gaps since they'd last seen each other. They finally got around to discussing what might happen next in this giant humanity-eating war.

"Scuttlebutt has it that we are headed next to an island called Iwo Jima," Howery said. Holloway had never heard of it. He looked around at the other men—they looked back with blank faces. It meant nothing to them. Before the war Holloway had never heard of Tulagi, Guadalcanal, Tarawa, Saipan, Guam, and now Iwo Jima. One thing was certain, he was getting a heck of a geography lesson.

Early in February, 1945, the Marines were ordered to board ship. They would, indeed be going to Iwo Jima. But Holloway's orders were different. Instead of shipping out, he was assigned to rear echelon. That meant that he would stay in Hawaii and keep track of the property for his unit. The Lieutenant in charge was the Battery Commander, and he assigned Holloway to the position of second in charge. Temporarily, he would be acting as a 1st Sergeant. The Rear Echelon group was camped on the edge of Hilo, Hawaii. They had quite a bit of spare time, which they spent partying in town. Holloway got used to hearing the men come staggering in late at night or in the early morning hours, singing "Don't Fence Me In." One night as Holloway was patrolling the camp, walking up and down the "streets", a gunshot rang out. He hustled over to that area, and could hear laughter coming from one of the tents. Apparently, there had been a fly in the tent and, when it landed on the ceiling, one of the

Marines shot it with a rifle. Holloway rebuked them for putting a hole in the tent, to say nothing of the danger of discharging a firearm in camp. He didn't think he should have to instruct them on the efficiency of using a fly swatter.

Cpl.. John P. Soares, Jr.
H&S Btry, 2nd 155 mm
Howitzer Bn
F.P.O. San Francisco
March 2, 1945

Hi there Pal,

Just droping you a few lines on one of these lousy V-mail to let you know that your partner is still kicking. Besides gaining a little weight. Life hasn't been to (sic) bad here, this new "C Ration" tops them all, even 10 in one. Also been having plenty of juices and canned fruits. The Japs, every once in awhile they let things go in this direction but we do our best to keep out of the way. The other day, Gregory seen Howery. But he didn't get a chance to talk to him very much because they were moving. Our gear got here in the best of condition. The only thing we forgot was tolit (sic) paper but that isn't holding the war. Old Stein said we were suppose to bring 6 boxes, that was the first time I knew that. No worry, we are making out swell. This island of Iwo Jima is pretty quiet tonight, for the present anyway.—Well Pal, take it easy and keep it clean

Your buddy—
Johnny
John P. Soares, Jr.

Being assigned to rear echelon kept a person out of the battle, but it didn't entirely remove one from the pain of death. The Lieutenant called Holloway in and told him to get Mitchell's gear together; he had been killed on Iwo Jima. The Lieutenant knew that Mitchell was a friend of Holloway's and that they had been through a lot together. Now Mitchell's belongings were to be shipped back to his family. The Lieutenant would write a note to them, hoping to let them know that others shared their grief. He was going through the dead Marine's gear, looking to take out anything that might hurt the family, as he told Holloway how it had happened. Somehow, Galbrist had gotten out in the open and was pinned down. It didn't look good for him. The Japs had a good line of sight. Galbrist started screaming for help, for someone to rescue him. The other Marines knew it was hopeless. To attempt a rescue would be to sacrifice their lives. There was only one man with the reckless bravado to try. Mitchell ran from shelter, into the open. If at all possible, he was going to rescue Galbrist. But he didn't make it; he was cut down as he reached the downed Marine. Both of them were killed.

Holloway felt emptiness inside him. He knew that Mitchell had all kinds of courage—maybe too much. That damned Galbrist! He'd been a pain in the butt since day one and now he'd gotten Mitchell killed. Holloway wondered how Mike Aaron was taking it. Aaron and Mitchell

"Marines start laying low.

Iwo Jima, Christina, 19 Feb 1945"

"The landing on Iwo Jima—H plus 1 hours Marine [sic]hug black volcanic sand as enemy machin [sic] guns, mortar whizz overhead.

SSgt.Bob Cooke Feb 1945"

were best buddies—inseparable. They must have been there together when Mitchell took that last dash to death.

One thing that was a constant in the military during wartime was that you were always being moved around. Holloway was moved to Honolulu, on the island of Oahu. That's where Hickam airfield was located, and Holloway was there expecting to get his orders to go elsewhere. It had been rumored that the next stop for his unit would be Okinawa. With Holloway was Corporal Freeman; both Marines were anxious to find out where they would be going next. As Holloway looked across the tarmac, lo and behold, just a short distance away was Captain Rouse, from his unit. Why wasn't he at Iwo Jima? He decided to find out. Walking up to him and saluting, he said, "Hello, sir. I thought you were at Iwo Jima." The Captain told him that their outfit was breaking up. That meant possibly going home, even if only temporarily. The Captain was certainly going home. Holloway felt a surge of excitement run through him—going home? He had his and Freeman's papers with him, detailing where they had been and what they had done. All it would take would be a quick okay from the Captain and they would be headed home too. Holloway held the papers out to Captain Rouse, "Can you see that we get transferred home now, sir?" Rouse looked at the papers, but he kept his hands at his sides. He looked away, gazing at the horizon. "Boys, I've got a plane to catch and I don't have time to monkey around with this." Translation: I won't lift a finger to help you guys get home. I am going home and that's all I care about. But Holloway wasn't going to give up. He walked over to the office of a Sergeant Major. As he and Freeman walked in, the Sergeant Major was busy with the paperwork to line up reserves to send to Okinawa. He looked up and asked what he could do for them. Holloway told him they were requesting to be sent home, and he held out their papers to the Sergeant Major. The officer sighed heavily, then reluctantly took the papers. He glanced at them, started to give them back, then looked at them some more, very closely, before exclaiming, "This is ridiculous!" Yes, it was ridiculous, thought Holloway. He and Freeman had been assaulting islands all over the Pacific, and they were about to be asked to do more of the same. The Sergeant Major looked up from the papers at the two Marines and said, "You will be aboard ship tonight!" They were going home! Back to the States!

Before he got on the ship, Holloway had to decide what he would take with him. He knew that when they disembarked in the States they could confiscate anything they wanted. Holloway had with him, among other things, a Japanese nambu machine gun and a knee mortar. Figuring the chances for confiscation were pretty high, he sold these. He also had a case of cigarettes, which he decided to take with him.

The trip back to San Diego was uneventful; Holloway was sick the entire way. As they pulled into the harbor, Holloway felt elated. He wanted to announce his joy at being back, and he did, along with others, by shouting "Home Alive, in '45!" Getting off the ship, they had to go through a shakedown at the Marine base. That's where they confiscated all his cigarettes. Another Marine in the group laid out a nambu machine gun with his gear. They had no problem with that—he got to keep it. Holloway kicked himself. If he had only kept his! That nambu would have made a great memento. But Holloway had kept his cigarettes, thinking they would have a better chance of making it through than a machine gun. He had been wrong.

Back in San Diego, Holloway went through Drill Instructor School and became a D.I.. It was easy. The new recruits had to know certain specific things and those things were drilled into them from early morning until late at night. Their dreams would be review lessons of what they needed to know. In addition, they had to go through all of the physical training—get rid of the fat and put on some muscle. Holloway had no qualms about doing the physical part right along with the recruits. He was in top shape. The drill instructor's life at the recruit depot fell into certain routines. They would get the guys up, get them fed, and exercise them until their tongues were hanging out. Then another D.I. would relieve him. The rest of the time was spent hanging out, meeting with the other D.I.s and comparing notes over donuts, or taking care of personal business, like doing your laundry (to wash clothes they used a scrub brush and a bar of soap). The recruits assigned to Holloway were a pretty alert bunch of boys. They didn't give him any problems.

Holloway was back in the States, but he knew he could be sent back into action at any time. The Japanese didn't act as if they wanted to give up any time soon. So he spent his time being a drill instructor and waiting for those next orders that could come at any time. One of his first days off he left the recruit depot, en route to probably the zoo, when he realized he was out of cigarettes. No problem, he stepped into a bar and, when he got the barmaid's attention, he asked for a pack of cigarettes. She stared back at him with a disgusted look on her face, then she put him in his place with, "We don't have any cigarettes! Don't you know there's a war on?!" She wheeled around and walked back to the other end of the bar. Yes, Holloway did know there was a war on. He had just spent close to four years in that war, four years that had grabbed him by the throat and would not relinquish that grip for many more years. But he didn't say anything to that barmaid. What could he say? She wouldn't understand.

The first extended leave found Holloway headed home to see his folks. Holloway jumped on the San Joaquin Daylight, a California train that traveled only in daylight hours, and headed north. At the end of that line he caught another train that would take him to Salem, Oregon. The train didn't have a diner car and the stops were few and brief. At one stop Holloway hustled over to a small café hoping to grab a bite to eat. He walked in the door to find the place jammed with people and the poor waitresses running to try to keep up. He did find a spot at the counter, but it didn't look like he would have time to eat. A commotion at one of the tables caught his attention and he heard a dissatisfied customer exclaim "You brought me the wrong thing. I didn't order that!" That was Holloway's opportunity. He raised his voice to be heard above the din and said to the waitress "Just bring it over here. I'll take it." It turned out to be the best hot beef sandwich he had ever tasted. His timing was impeccable. He had a quick but delicious meal and trotted back to the station just before the train pulled out.

When the train arrived in Salem, Oregon, Holloway called a friend in Amity who had a telephone (his parents didn't) and asked her to have his folks pick him up. He was waiting for them at the train station. Mom and Dad hugged their boy, and they all cried. Stan had been gone for almost four years, most of it kept secret from his parents; communication with home was censored to not reveal where their son was. But now they had their Stan home. Mom called Beulah and Will Patty, their close friends and neighbors, and told them the news. Then the Pattys came over and they had a big dinner to celebrate Stan's homecoming.

Farmington, Wash.
June 5, 1945

Dear Margaret:

Well, here we are in Farmington for about ten days —
and Stan is with us. A week ago Friday night he telephoned
Dorothy Burns (we have no telephone) that he was in Salem,
"please tell Mother to come get me." Needless to say we were on
our way in no time and I never saw the miles go so slowly.
When we neared the depot there he was waiting for us and how
good it seemed to hug him tight to me and know he was mine
for at least thirty days. He looks well only is terribly tanned
and nervous, but oh so happy to be home. Last Friday Dad,
he, and I started for Washington. We drove over in my car. We
came over the Columbia River Highway. Scotch Broom lined
the highway in Oregon and syringa the Washington roads.
The folks Uncle Plut and Aunt Mildred were very happy to
see him. They are in Spokane today buying Stan's "blues",
Mildred's shoes and Plut's "dyes"— something he uses in
carpenter work. Dad and I stayed home. We have been staying
up late, so thought we would catch up on our rest. I am at
home here for this was my home before I was married. My
father and brother built the house.

Stan has told us so much about you it seems as if we
almost knew you. He seems so proud of you. Margaret, I want
to love you— I do love you now, but be sure Stan is the only
man before you come. The papers are all made out. You are a
girl brought up in a big city; can you come and live on a farm

and work hard and be happy? Can you live so far from your loved ones and be happy?

Stan loves you more than any one but even he gets irritable sometimes. U.S. is a wonderful country but we live hard and fast. I haven't a doubt but Stan can make a good living for you if they ever release him. He has 30 days here and 6 months in the U.S. Then what? He wants you now—I would rather in some ways he was home for good first so he could be right with you, but you and he will have to settle that.

I made him a pumpkin pie this A.M. and am ready now to make some raised doughnuts.

Love to you and your mother.
Mother Holloway

In San Diego, some of Holloway's cronies would party it up when they had a day off, but Holloway felt the need for solitude. He found that solitude at the San Diego Zoo. As soon as he entered the front gates he could feel himself relax. There was so much to see and watch! Holloway could sit on a bench and watch the animals and forget for a while the things that reared their ugly heads throughout the world. Maybe it's because animals don't seem to harbor hatred and animosity that watching them, even in repose, can be cathartic and relaxing. Some of the animals amazed him—he had always thought eagles were very big birds, but then he saw the turkey buzzard, with an eight-foot wing span. And polar bears had always seemed big to him, until he saw a Kodiak grizzly bear. Holloway never got tired of the zoo.

On August 6th, 1945, the United States dropped an atomic bomb on the Japanese city of Hiroshima. Three days later another atomic bomb was dropped on the city of Nagasaki. That did it. There would be no invasion of Japan. The Japanese surrendered unconditionally and

Emperor Hirohito announced defeat to his people on August 14th, 1945. The war was over. Everyone celebrated. Holloway knew that he would be headed home as soon as he could get his walking papers. But first the Marine Corps would court him into possibly staying in the service for a while longer. They called him into an office at the recruit depot. There were several recruiting officers there. They were friendly; they had a sales pitch for him—if he would sign up for four more years... Holloway didn't say anything, he let them continue their spiel, but he was thinking (I just want to go home). "You would receive an advancement in rank, maybe Sergeant or Staff Sergeant." (Four more years of putting up with all kinds of bullshit from officers?) "You would also receive an increase in pay." (Where's the door? Would they get the message if I ran out of here?)

"What do you think, Holloway?"

"I just want to get out." That's all he said. There was no more discussion. He was dismissed.

But that wasn't the end of proposals he would get. Law officers from all over California tried to recruit the Marines that weren't staying. The job offers looked pretty good, with good pay and security. Holloway wanted nothing to do with any of it. He didn't want to wear a uniform any more. He didn't want to pack a firearm anymore. And he damn sure didn't want to take orders from anyone, especially someone in uniform. He was going home. As soon as he received his discharge papers, Stan packed up his gear and traveled to Amity. The Marine Corps was in his past, not forgotten but not consciously brought to mind unless some old incident or memory jumped out of the past like a scary figure in a haunted house ride. Most of the time he kept them at bay, but sometimes things would come back in his sleep and he would find himself back in the water at Tarawa or crouched in the middle of a mortar barrage at Saipan. When awakened in the middle of the night, Stan would put on his robe and slippers and amble to the kitchen. While waiting for the kettle to boil for a cup of tea, he would stare out the window. He was alive and living not only for himself and his family, but also for those who didn't make it. He would never forget them.

Stan went to work right away for Newman Painting, painting post offices, some as far away as Chico, California, Phoenix, Arizona, and Orofino, Idaho. He enjoyed the work and was able to put most of the war memories behind him. Then, after being home about six months he received an official looking letter from the U.S. Marine Corps. In the letter it stated that upon review of his payroll while in the service it had come to their attention that Stan Holloway had been over-paid by $63.27. Please remit promptly.

Stan laughed. He crumpled up the letter and threw it in the trash. What could they possibly be thinking? Wasn't it enough that he'd put his butt on the line and had endured all kinds of hell for four years? They had received their pound of flesh and now they were asking for more. It was ludicrous.

Several months went by before Stan received the second letter. This one was more demanding and threatened to send military police to pick him up if they did not receive payment from him. He would have to serve time in the Marine Corps to pay for the $63.27 he owed them. Stan went to the bank, made out a certified check to the U.S. Marine Corps for $63.27 and promptly sent it.

Margaret Stewart— Stan carried this picture in his wallet during the war.

Epilogue

*I*t was 1946, the war was over, and Stan and Margaret wanted to get married. But getting Marg to the States was an endeavor that was fraught with red tape and bureaucratic foot dragging. When Stan walked away from the Marine Corps he also unintentionally stopped the progress of the system to get Marg on a ship. The Marines turned all the paperwork over to the Red Cross. New forms were required to be filled out by Stan and his parents. His folks had to provide financial statements proving that they could support the new immigrant if they had to. The government did not want people coming into the country and becoming destitute, whereby it would fall on Uncle Sam to support them.

Marg had filled out the necessary paperwork on her end, received a passport, and underwent a medical exam. The next step was to get permission to board a ship going to the States that would accommodate passengers, which wasn't easy because ships were in short supply. However, after waiting for several months, one became available. The name of the vessel was the "Rangitiki." Coincidentally, Marg had been born in Rangitiki Province, and she felt it was a good omen for the long trip. The Rangitiki was commissioned to carry both freight and passengers, which included about 100 New Zealand women who were either married or engaged to U.S. servicemen.

Once on board ship, Marg wondered how she would do with sea travel. She'd never been on the ocean before, but hoped she would take after her father's side of the family, who enjoyed traveling by sea. Early in the voyage Marg had one day of seasickness. The constant rocking motion hypnotized her

147

body into thinking it would come apart from the inside. So she went on deck and let the fresh salt-laced air blow across her face and through her loose shoulderlength hair until the queasiness gradually subsided.

The ship had a final destination of England, by way of the Panama Canal, with a stop at Newport News, Virginia, to unload passengers. However, there was a shipping strike on the east coast which prohibited the ship from docking at Newport News, or their secondary option of New York city. They continued north to Nova Scotia.

Meanwhile, Holloway was trying to work with immigration officials and the Red Cross. He was required to pay a bond to show good faith in supporting Marg and to cover the expense of sending her back to New Zealand if anything went wrong. Stan was first told that his fiancée couldn't get off the ship until the bond was paid and presented. Then other officials told him that they could not present the bond until after she had disembarked. By that time the officials also had no idea where the ship would dock. The bureaucratic mis-information was driving Holloway mad. He finally went to the bonding company, USF&G, and talked to a very helpful lady who assured him, "Wherever that ship docks, we will have the bond there. Everything will be fine." She was like an island of sense and understanding in a sea of wrong answers and apathy.

As the Rangitiki pulled into the Halifax harbor, the young N.Z. women were fidgeting with excitement. Some of their husbands/fiancés had driven up to meet them. The girls had had a delightful time on the voyage, getting acquainted with one another, relaxing together, and partying. (There was a men's rugby team from England on board, which added to the fun.) But now they were to enter another life by simply stepping off the ship.

As the girls looked across to the distant dock, they could see some of the men wearing zoot suits. One of the girls said, "If my fiancé is wearing a zoot suit, I'll just die!" Later, on the dock, Marg saw that the girl had found her man, and he was festooned in a zoot suit. Marg caught a train to New York City and checked into a hotel. The Red Cross directed her to a train that would leave right away to take her west. But Marg had other ideas. She found the city to be exhilarating and decided to stay for five days. One of the other N.Z. girls joined Marg for the final two days before they left for their respective destinations of

Oregon and Texas. (The other girl had been engaged to a serviceman from Texas, but he married another girl before she left N.Z. She cancelled her plans, but the young man's parents had come to love her through their correspondence and persuaded her to come anyway. She wrote to Marg afterwards telling her what happened. The parents welcomed her into their home and were very pleased to have her there. Just after she arrived, the son came over. He didn't know she was coming, and when he saw her he stood there and cried. She did enjoy her stay with the parents but then went back to N.Z.)

Marg took in as much as she could of New York, enjoying the Rockettes and seeing the Empire State Building, among other things. On Fifth Avenue she went into a shoe store and struck up a conversation with a nice young man who, coincidentally, was from Salem, Oregon. He said his father owned a shoe store and suggested Marg drop in and say "Hi" when she got to Salem. Some time later, Marg and Stan did drop by and introduce themselves to the shop owner in Salem. He was very gracious and extremely pleased to meet them. Marg and Stan always remembered him saying to them, "If you get any traffic tickets in this town, let me know. I'll take care of them."

Stan was beside himself. He had lost Marg. The Red Cross had no idea where she was. He and his brother in law, Bill Rice, drove in to the Immigration Office in Portland to see if they could help locate Marg. Stan asked the man behind the counter for assistance and was told, "That's not my department. We can't help you here." Having dismissed these people, he started to turn away. Holloway was angry. He shouted "Whose department is it?" Bill could see that things might escalate. If the immigration man gave a sarcastic or calloused answer, Holloway might vault the counter. He said, "What's your name? Your head office is in Philadelphia isn't it?" The man looked from Stan's glaring eyes to Bill and realized this was a divergence from his normal routine. He said, "Maybe I can help you." Then he bustled around, made some inquiries, and did assist them. They hadn't pinpointed Marg's location, but they were able to trace her steps somewhat. Meanwhile, Marg had written a letter to Stan telling of her plans in New York, but the letter was delayed in the mail.

It was mid-August, 1946, when the train pulled into Portland, Oregon. Stan was waiting in his best suit. Marg stepped from the train, spotted him, and ran into his arms. Her light cotton dress flared as he twirled her— they *kissed for a long time. Stan grabbed her luggage and led Marg out of the station and to his well-polished, tan 1941 Plymouth. It had lots of glittering chrome and ran like a Swiss watch. But he didn't stop at his car. He, instead, walked up to an old junker with one end of the front bumper held on with bailing wire. The driver-side door was missing and the entire car was splattered with mud.*

They stood beside the car. In a soft voice, Marg said, "Is this your car?" After a short pause, Stan said, "Actually, no. Mine's over here." And he started walking back to his car. They were both laughing and Marg uttered an exclamation that she would say many times over the years. "Oh, Stan!"

Columbus Day, October 12, 1946, Stanley P. Holloway and Margaret D. Stewart were married in Amity, Oregon. Stan pulled a buggy cart down Main Street and Marg sat in the seat, brandishing a buggy whip, her white satin marriage gown flowing behind her. Friends and family lined the street and cheered them on.

Mr. And Mrs. Stan Holloway moved to Farmington, Washington, and farmed wheat, lentils, barley, and peas. They raised a family of two girls and two boys. In 1970 they quit farming and went to work at Washington State University, from where they both retired. They now live in Pullman, Washington.

Stan and Margaret Holloway   1998

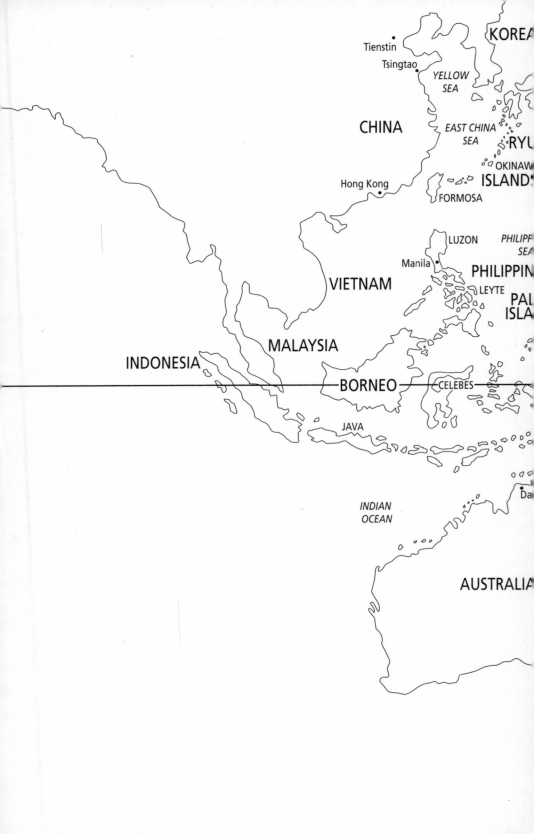